Doodle Stitching
THE HOLIDAY MOTIF
COLLECTION

Doodle Stitching

THE HOLIDAY MOTIF COLLECTION

Embroidery Projects & Designs to Celebrate the Seasons

AIMEE RAY

LARK

An Imprint of Sterling Publishing
387 Park Avenue South
New York, NY 10016

ISBN 978-1-4547-0859-9

Library of Congress Cataloging-in-Publication Data

Ray, Aimee, 1976-
  Doodle stitching. The holiday motif collection embroidery projects &
designs to celebrate the seasons / Aimee Ray.
     pages cm
  Includes bibliographical references and index.
  ISBN 978-1-4547-0859-9 (alk. paper)
  1. Embroidery--Patterns. 2. Stitches (Sewing) 3. Holiday decorations.
I. Title.
  TT771.R3728 2014
  746.44--dc23
                                          2014005835

Distributed in Canada by Sterling Publishing
c/o Canadian Manda Group, 165 Dufferin Street
Toronto, Ontario, Canada M6K 3H6
Distributed in the United Kingdom by GMC Distribution Services
Castle Place, 166 High Street, Lewes, East Sussex, England BN7 1XU
Distributed in Australia by Capricorn Link (Australia) Pty. Ltd.
P.O. Box 704, Windsor, NSW 2756, Australia

For information about custom editions, special sales, and premium and corporate purchases, please
contact Sterling Special Sales at 800-805-5489 or specialsales@sterlingpublishing.com.

Email academic@larkbooks.com for information about desk and examination copies. The complete
policy can be found at larkcrafts.com.

Manufactured in China

2 4 6 8 10 9 7 5 3 1

larkcrafts.com

CONTENTS

INTRODUCTION

Happy Doodle Stitching Holidays! I hope that opening this book feels like opening a gift. I had so much fun making it, and I think that's because, for me, holidays and creating go together. Holidays are when we make memories, so it's the perfect time to make keepsakes. I love to give handmade gifts because they feel so much more personal than something from the mall. And decorating my house with things I've stitched up myself makes celebrating especially fun and meaningful. Of course, like everyone else, I never have enough time at the holidays. Luckily, doodle stitching, my free-form type of embroidery, is so easy, fun, inexpensive, and versatile that it can fit into your holiday schedule and your budget.

But I do need to warn you: Just like those goodies that you can't stop eating between Thanksgiving and New Year's Day, doodle stitching is addictive. Once you start, you'll want to stitch everything in sight. Luckily, this book and the CD in the back contain over 300 motifs for Christmas and holidays throughout the year. Turn the pages and you'll find traditional Christmas imagery like snowflakes, reindeer, holly, and trees, as well as fresh, unique designs inspired by the Nutcracker, candy land, and vintage ornaments. And then you'll find pages of motifs for an entire year of holidays! The CD holds every motif in digital form so you can enlarge, edit, and combine motifs for any project you can dream up. If you don't feel like dreaming up something on your own, this book offers step-by-step instructions to help you create 21 projects perfect for the winter holidays. Some of the projects are my own designs, and others were designed by six super-talented designers: Annie Kight, Carina Envoldsen-Harris, John Q. Adams, Laura Howard, Mollie Johanson, and Teresa Mairal Barreu. I'm really excited for you to discover you favorite motifs, colors, and stitch combinations and dive into these pages.

Is your heart a lot fuller than your wallet this year? Raid your fabric and floss stash and stitch up something personal and unique, like the Frolicking Foxes Lap Quilt or the Noel Wall Hanging. Are you in too much of a hurry to make an entire gift from scratch? Personalize store-bought items to make the Snowflake Slippers or the Sleepy Mouse Pillowcase. This book is a gift intended to keep on giving: You can easily swap motifs to make some of these projects work for other holidays, such as slippers for Mother's Day or even a wall hanging for Halloween. You won't get cavities or calories from embroidery, so doodle on, dear readers—my goal is to keep you in stitches the whole year through.

—Aimee

EMBROIDERY ESSENTIALS

In a world that has become increasingly full of gadgets and gizmos, and more and more commercial when it comes to the holidays, the simplicity of embroidery appeals to me. I love that anyone can create something beautiful with just a needle, floss, a hoop, and some fabric. Of course, there are a few other items that will come in handy when embroidering and a few techniques to get the hang of. But embroidery is one of the easiest crafts to learn, and doodle stitching is all about play and freedom—no need to count stitches or decipher confusing codes! This section of the book will teach you embroidery basics to get started, and the Sewing Essentials on page 21 will be handy in projects that follow. Some of the projects use quilt-making techniques, and you'll find tips for those starting on page 23.

MATERIALS & TOOLS

Floss

I'm like a kid on Christmas morning when it comes to floss. The variety of colors available is truly astonishing. Floss is sold in small bundles, or skeins. Each strand of floss is made up of six threads, or plies, twisted together. For a thick embroidered line, use all six threads. For smaller, more delicate work, separate the threads and use fewer. I use either six or three threads for most embroidery projects. If I'm hand-sewing fabric together and using floss instead of sewing thread, I'll usually use one thread of floss.

Standard cotton floss is most common, but there are also many specialty flosses available, such as metallic, linen, silk, and gradient colors, which are fun to play with. (The Felt Star Tree Topper, below and on page 51, makes good use of metallic floss.)

No one has ever accused me of being a neat freak, but I do love to organize. When my creative space and supplies are arranged so that I can easily see and find everything, I feel much more inspired to make things and use all the crafty stuff I've collected. There are lots of ways to organize your floss and lots of products on the market to help you.

Each skein of embroidery floss comes wrapped in paper with a different number for each color. When you unwrap a new skein of floss, keep track of that important number on the package. With hundreds of different floss colors, it's easy to forget the exact shade of aqua you were using. I can tell you from personal experience that it's frustrating try to match colors from memory or that little length of floss in

EMBROIDERY TOOLBOX

Embroidery hoop (a 6-inch [15.2 cm] circle is a good one to start with)

Embroidery and sewing needles

Embroidery floss

Fabric stabilizer

Iron

Nonpermanent fabric pen

Sewing scissors

Straight pins

Thimble

Transfer or tracing materials and tools

Tweezers

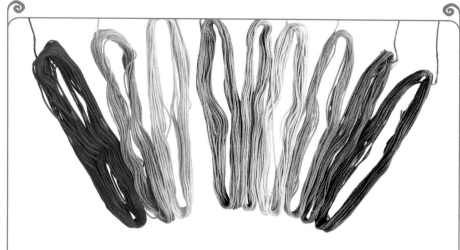

HOLIDAY COLORS

I often get asked what colors I've used in my embroidery art. I use DMC brand floss, and each color is labeled with a number. If you use a different brand of floss, you can search the internet for a color conversion chart that will give you the equivalent numbers to these. Here is a list of my favorite colors, and the ones I used for the projects in this book:

Pink: dark 760, medium 761, light 3713

Cherry Red: 321/304

Coral: dark 350 through light 353

Coral Red: 349

Orange: dark 720, medium 721, light 722

Yellow-orange: 3854

Yellow: 727

Pale Green: dark 3346 through light 3348

Bright Green: dark 905, medium 906, light 907

Aqua: medium 3811, light 747

Turquoise: dark 3810, medium 597, light 598

Blue: dark 340, medium 341/157, light 3747

Plum: dark 3834, medium 3835, light 3836

Brown: dark 433 through light 437

Yellow-brown: medium 676, light 422

Ecru

Black: 310

White: Blanc

your purse. Instead, make it easy by winding your floss onto a cardboard bobbin and writing the number on the bobbin. Here is the template I use to make mine.

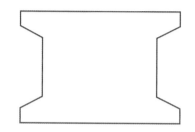

I keep all my floss bobbins in a clear plastic tackle box, arranged by color. I have one extra slot in the box for leftover floss pieces that are too long to throw away, and another for my scissors and a small pincushion with pins and needles. I can easily close the box up and put it away when I'm not using it (though usually it sits open on the couch in the living room, along with my current project) or even take it with me to use on the road.

Needles

You don't really need a special type or size of needle for embroidering. All you really need is one with a sharp point and a hole, or "eye," that's large enough for you to thread floss through easily. Use a needle with a larger eye if you're using all six threads of floss, and one with a small eye if you're using three or fewer or hand-sewing with thread. I buy packs of several different sizes of needles so I have a variety to choose from. Keep a small pincushion close by so your needles won't get lost. You can easily make one of any shape or size by hand-sewing two pieces of felt together with a little stuffing inside. Don't forget to decorate it with embroidery!

Thimble

A thimble will make gripping and pushing the needle through the fabric like canvas or denim much easier on your fingers. Besides, you'll feel so domesticated when you use one!

Embroidery Hoops

Although you can embroider some heavy, thick fabrics without a hoop, most fabrics will require one. Hooping your fabric will give you a tight, smooth surface to stitch on, and it will prevent puckering. Embroidery hoops consist of two round frames that fit together and tighten with a screw. The frames hold your fabric taut as you stitch. They come in plastic or wood and many different sizes. Plastic hoops are a good investment; they are sturdier than wood and will last a long time. You can use different sized hoops for different sized projects, but I've found a 6-inch (15.2 cm) one works well for almost anything.

Scissors

Any pair of scissors will do, but it's nice to have a small pair of sharp sewing scissors that you can keep with your embroidery floss and supplies.

Fabric and Other Materials

Here's my rule for fabric: if you can stick a needle through it, you can embroider it! The most common, and the fabric used for many of the projects in this book, is quilter's cotton. Felt, canvas, denim, and satin are also great fabrics to embroider on. Nothing is safe around my house when holidays are near and I have floss and needle in hand. Embroidery is such an easy way to add a seasonal touch to towels, pillowcases, curtains, sweaters, and sweatshirts.

And you don't need to stop at fabrics—I certainly don't. Heavy paper, vinyl, thin plastics, and even balsa wood can also be embroidered. To stitch on balsa wood, first apply a layer of white craft glue and a thin cotton fabric to the back to prevent cracking. When stitching on wood or paper, poke holes from the front first to come through from the back. It's best to stick with simpler stitches, and not to pull through so tightly that the paper rips or balsa wood cracks. With a little extra care, you can make lots of unique projects with embroidery on these surfaces.

Stabilizer

Use a fabric stabilizer when embroidering on stretchy or delicate fabrics such as T-shirt cotton or silk: it will keep the fabric from stretching as you work to help make a smoother finished product. Stabilizer comes in many varieties. The type I use most is the tear-away paper kind with an adhesive back. You can easily cut it to whatever size or shape you need, stick it onto the back of your fabric, and even remove and reposition it if necessary. You embroider right through the paper and fabric together. When you're done, just gently tear away the excess and use tweezers or the tip of your needle to remove any bits of paper caught under the stitches. For delicate fabrics, I use a water-soluble stabilizer that easily dissolves in water once I'm done embroidering.

TRANSFERRING PATTERNS

Okay, transferring patterns is not the most enjoyable part of the process. But over the years I've found several different methods to do so, depending on the different types of fabric I'm transferring the pattern to. Experiment with the list that follows to find the best match for you and your fabric (it's a good idea to test any fabric pens or iron-on prints on a piece of scrap fabric before trying them out on your actual project).

Light Method

My old standby method is to trace patterns using a light table or a sunny window. I simply tape the pattern to a light table or window and secure the fabric over it so the pattern lines show through the fabric. My favorite tools for tracing pattern lines onto fabric are water-soluble fabric markers. Fabric-marker lines are easy to remove with

water when you're done embroidering. An ordinary pencil will work, too, although it is more difficult to remove, so be sure to cover lead pencil lines completely with your embroidery. The light table or sunny-window method works best for lightweight, light-colored fabrics.

Carbon Paper Method

Another way to transfer patterns to fabric is by using fabric carbon paper. You can find it in most fabric and craft stores. It comes in a variety of colors to contrast with the color of fabric you're using. Place your fabric on a hard surface, set a piece of carbon paper facedown on top of it, and your pattern on top of that. Trace the pattern lines with a pencil or other blunt object, such as a knitting needle. I use this method mostly for darker-colored fabrics that marker lines don't show up on.

Iron-On Transfers

A third method is to make an iron-on transfer. Just use a black-and-white laser print or photocopy of any design (unfortunately, prints from ink-jet printers won't work). Place the print on top of your fabric facedown and iron it to transfer the image onto the fabric. Remember, especially if your pattern includes text, that you'll need to reverse the image before printing

it or it will be backward when you apply it to your fabric. The lines will be permanent, though they may fade with washing or over time, so you'll need to cover them completely with your embroidery. Homemade iron-on transfers can vary greatly depending on the type of paper, ink, and fabric you're using, so you may need to experiment a bit with this method.

Tissue Paper Method

One of my favorite transferring techniques (especially when working with thick fabrics like felt) is to trace the pattern onto thin paperlike tissue or tracing paper, pin the paper to the fabric, and stitch right through the paper and the fabric together. When you're done, just tear away the paper. Use tweezers or the tip of your needle to remove any bits of paper caught under the stitches.

CHOOSING & USING MOTIFS

The CD included with this book conveniently gives you all the motifs in digital form as black-and-white EPS files that can be modified to your needs and as JPEGs, which can be used just the way they are. Just pop it in your computer, read the helpful User Guide, and get started. You can resize the motifs in any image-editing program, print them out, and transfer them to your fabric using one of the methods described at left. Remember, if you're using the iron-on transfer method, you'll need to reverse your images first so they don't end up backward on your fabric. You will most often want to use black line art for easy transferring.

Because you have the motifs in digital form, it's easy to combine them to create your own unique patterns and designs. Don't worry, you won't hurt my feelings! Go ahead and resize, overlap, change colors, omit elements, or draw in your own additions to make a pattern distinctly yours. If you're proficient with an image program, you can design your own motif combinations digitally before printing them, trying out lots of different colors and layout options. If you're better with paper and scissors, print and cut out your favorite motifs and arrange them by hand, collage style.

And keep in mind that the colors in the book and the stitches listed for the motifs used in the projects are just recommendations. If you lean toward red instead of pink, go for it. If you want to vary stitches to add extra details or textures that may not be included in the pattern, be my guest. I often improvise at the stitching stage, which is one reason I like to use removable fabric markers: that way, I'm free to change my mind as I work and can easily remove any pattern lines left over when I'm finished.

GET STITCHING!

Okay, you've chosen your motifs, transferred your pattern to the fabric, and applied stabilizer (if needed)—now it's time to hoop your fabric. Simply place the fabric over the inside frame of an embroidery hoop and slip the outer frame on top, fitting them together. Tighten the screw and gently pull the edges of the fabric until it's taut.

Next, choose a color of floss, cut a length about 12 inches (30.5 cm) long, and thread your needle. If it resists going through the needle's eye, try dampening one end of the floss and twisting it to a point. Tie a knot in the other end of the floss. One way to tie a knot is to wrap it around your finger, roll it off, and pull downward to tighten it.

needle under a stitch, looping it, and pulling it tight. Snip off the extra floss and start again.

You can work on your embroidery section by section, completing each area before moving on to the next one, or stitch a single color throughout the design before moving on to the next color.

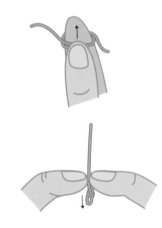

Now, you are ready to start embroidering! Pull the needle and floss through from the back of your fabric until the knot catches. Choose a stitch and follow the pattern's lines. When you finish a line or color section of embroidery stitches, or you get down to about 2 inches (5.1 cm) of floss, tie a small knot on the back by slipping your

THE EYES HAVE IT

This little trick to make your embroidered eyes look realistic is called for in a few of the projects. The stitches (shown below) are essentially just three satin stitches (usually in black) with a white highlight added in.

Watch Your Back

I'm not too fussy when embroidering on thick fabrics or making projects where the back of the embroidery will be hidden. You will want to keep the back of your embroidery neat if it will be visible, such as on a dish towel, or on very thin, light-colored fabrics where messy knots or tails of floss can show through the fabric. To keep the backs of your embroidery looking neat, tie knots tightly and close to the fabric, and snip off any extra floss right above the knot. Also, limit the distance you stretch your floss across the back from stitch to stitch. Tie off your floss with each section of the design and start with a new knot at the next point, rather than stretching your floss from point to point. I usually don't stretch my floss longer than ½ inch (1.3 cm); this reduces the "spiderweb" effect on the back.

Finishing

When you've finished your embroidery, remove the fabric from the hoop and erase any removable transfer lines by rinsing it with water or hand-washing it with a gentle detergent. Press the water out by spreading the fabric flat or rolling it between two towels. When it's almost dry, iron it facedown on a towel. This will remove any wrinkles but prevent crushing your stitches.

STITCH LIBRARY

Here are all the embroidery stitches you'll need to make the projects in this book.

Straight Stitch

The Straight Stitch is the most basic embroidery stitch. Just pull your needle through from the back at A and push it back down at B. Straight Stitches can be any length, from a tiny dot to a line about ¼ inch (6 mm) long. Make several Straight Stitches in a line to form the Running Stitch or in a circle pointing out from the center to make a flower shape. You can also stitch them individually or in groupings for small details like eyes or fur.

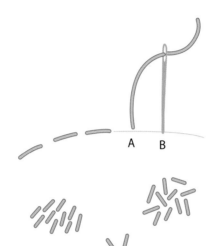

Cross Stitch

Start with a small diagonal Straight Stitch, from A to B. Make a second stitch over it from C to D. Rows of Cross Stitches look neater when the lines for each cross overlap in the same direction. If you're making a row, you can stitch a line of identical diagonal stitches, then go back and cross over them in the other direction.

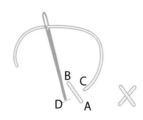

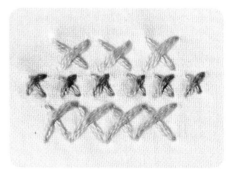

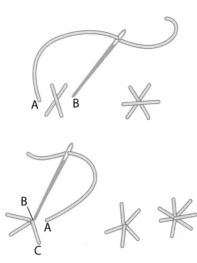

Star Stitch

Stars can be made in the same way as Cross Stitches. Start by making a Cross Stitch, and then add an additional Straight Stitch on top of it, from A to B.

Another way to make a Star is by making several Straight Stitches in a circle, ending at the same center point. Make your first stitch from A to B, your second stitch from C to B, and so on. Continue around the center, adding as many stitches as you like until you reach the first stitch.

Split Stitch

Split Stitched lines are quick and easy to make, and make great outlines.

Make a small Straight Stitch from A to B. Bring the needle back up at C, splitting the first stitch in half. Continue making stitches and splitting them, to form a line.

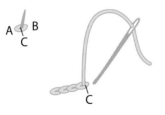

Stem Stitch

The Stem Stitch is perfect for stitching curved lines or flower stems, which is how it got its name. Make a stitch from A to B, leaving the floss a little loose. Pull the needle to the front again at C, between A and B and just to one side. Pull the floss tight and continue to form a line of stitches.

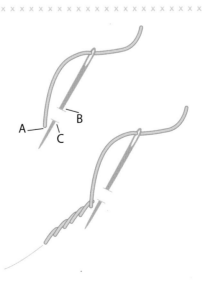

Back Stitch

The Back Stitch is a nice, clean outlining stitch. Start with a small stitch in the opposite direction, from A to B. Bring your needle back through the fabric at C, ahead of the first stitch and ending at A. Repeat to make each new Back Stitch, working backward on the surface and inserting the needle at the end of the previous stitch.

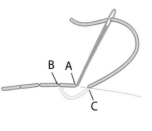

Chain Stitch

The Chain Stitch is great for a thick outline, but also works nicely as a decorative border. Pull the needle and floss through the fabric at A (figure 1). Insert the needle back in at A, pulling the floss through to the back until you have a small loop on the front. Bring the needle back up through the fabric inside of the loop at B (figure 2). Reinsert the needle at B, pulling the floss through to form a second small loop. Continue stitching loops to make a Chain (figure 3). When you finish a row, make a tiny stitch over the end of the last loop to hold it in place.

To end a Chain Stitch circle, stop one stitch short of the first stitch, and slide your needle and floss underneath it at C (figure 4). Then finish the last stitch, completing the circle.

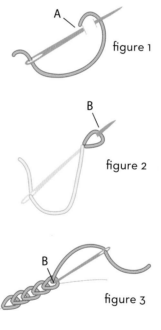

figure 1

figure 2

figure 3

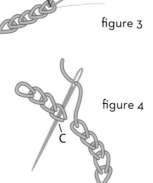

figure 4

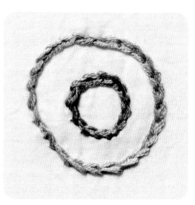

Blanket Stitch

The Blanket Stitch makes a great decorative border or edging. Make a loose, diagonal stitch from A to B. Bring the needle up again at C, catching the floss under the needle and pulling it tight to the fabric.

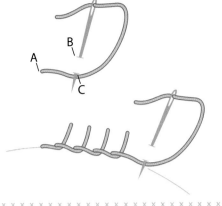

French Knot

French Knots can be tricky at first, but they are well worth taking the time to learn. Individually, they make great dot accents, or fill an area solidly with French Knots for an interesting texture. Bring the needle through the fabric at A. Wrap the floss around the tip of the needle in the direction shown, and reinsert the needle at B, right next to A. Pull the floss tight and close to the fabric as you pull the needle back through. You can make larger French Knots by wrapping the floss around the needle multiple times.

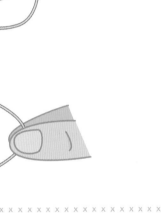

Lazy Daisy

The Lazy Daisy Stitch is the perfect way to make flower petals and leaves. You can use Satin Stitches or French Knots to make the flower centers. Bring your needle through the fabric at A and put it back down in the same spot, but don't pull the floss all the way through; leave a small loop. Now bring your needle back through the fabric inside the loop at B and back down at C, catching the loop at the top and securing it to the fabric. Repeat this stitch in a circle to make a daisy.

Fly Stitch

The Fly Stitch is an interesting decorative accent stitch and also makes cute flowers. Pair it with a Satin Stitch circle or French Knots to form the buds. Make a loose horizontal stitch from A to B. Press the loop flat to one side with your finger. Bring the needle back up at C, in the center of the first stitch. Return the needle at D, securing the first stitch to the fabric.

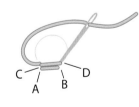

Scallop Stitch

The Scallop Stitch is a cousin to the Fly Stitch and Lazy Daisy and is made with the same basic technique. Scallop Stitches are also great for making flowers or leaves, or stitch several in a row to make a pretty border. Make a loose stitch from A to B and press it flat to one side with your finger. Bring the needle to the front of the fabric at C, inside the loop. Insert the needle at the outside of the stitch, at D, to hold it in place.

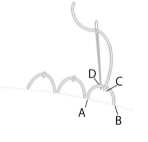

Satin Stitch

Satin Stitches are a lovely way to fill in small areas with smooth, solid color. Make a Straight Stitch from A to B. Make a second stitch right next to the first one from C to D. Always bring your needle up on one side and down on the other for best results. If you have trouble keeping the edges of your area even, first outline the shape with a tight Back Stitch or Split Stitch, and make your Satin Stitches over the top. For an extra smooth area of Satin Stitches, untwist and separate the threads of floss first.

SEWING ESSENTIALS

Many of the projects in this book can be sewn by hand. A few (such as the Frolicking Foxes Lap Quilt) call for a sewing machine. Here are a few of the sewing techniques used in the book's projects.

Hidden Stitch

A few of the projects in this book are sewn inside out, turned right side out through an unstitched opening (also called the "turning gap,") and then (for pieces like the Soft Nativity on page 44 or the Plush Vintage Ornaments on page 46) stuffed. The Hidden Stitch is a nearly invisible stitch you can used to close the opening. To do so, first fold the excess fabric in along each side of the opening and pin the hole closed. Thread a needle with thread matching the color of the fabric and knot it at one end. Bring the needle and thread through the fabric from the back at A and back down directly across the opening at B. Slide the needle along the inside of the fold and pull it back out at C, trapping the stitch inside. Reinsert the needle across from C at D, pulling

the thread tightly. Continue stitching along the opening, closing up the seam. When you get to the end, make a tiny knot buried in the seam.

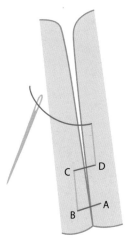

Topstitch

Topstitching is done by hand or machine after fabric pieces are sewn together and the project is turned right side out. Just sew a line of small Straight Stitches close together through both layers of fabric. Topstitching is usually done close to and parallel with an edge.

Slipstitch

If you don't want your stitches to show, the slipstitch is usually used when two hemmed or folded edges of fabrics are joined. It's useful for attaching bindings to quilts or for closing the gap in a stuffed project. Begin by inserting your threaded needle though from inside of a folded or hemmed edge, anchoring the knot inside the fabic. Insert the needle into opposite folded edge (if no fold, just pick up a few threads of the opposite fabric), then run the needle just a tiny distance inside the fold and poke the needle back into the top fold of the fabric and repeat.

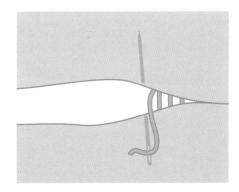

Whip Stitch

Whip Stitches are a great way to add a decorative touch while joining pieces of fabric together along matched edges. You can also use it to hem the raw edge of a piece of fabric (such as the felt appliqués in the Teashop Teapot Cozy on page 85), or alone as a decorative stitch. Use matching thread to hide your stitches, or embroidery floss in a contrasting color to show them off.

Starting at the back, or between two pieces of fabric, bring your needle and floss through at A. Bring the needle over the edge of the fabric and reinsert it from the back at B.

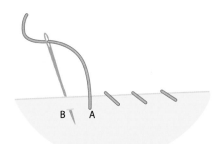

Stab Stitch

The Stab Stitch is a variation of the Running Stitch using very tiny stitches. It's most often used to attach a piece of fabric to a background fabric. Use thread matching the fabric or one thread from a strand of floss. Bring the needle up at A and down at B, ⅛ inch (3 mm) from the edge of the fabric. Continue stitching all around the edge.

Notching Edges and Trimming Corners

When making projects such as pillows or stuffed pieces, you will sew two pieces of fabric together with the right sides facing. Before you turn the fabric pieces right side out again, you will want to first "notch" the fabric around the seam so that the edges of your finished project look neat and smooth. For curved edges, cut small, triangular pieces out of the fabric, cutting right up to, but not through your stitched seam (figure 1). Make notches ½ to 1 inch (1.3 to 2.5 cm) apart. The tighter the curve, the more notches should be cut. Cut corners off straight across as shown (figure 2).

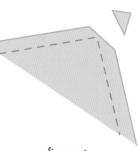

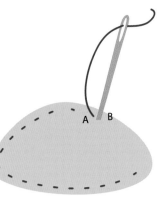

figure 1   figure 2

QUILTING ESSENTIALS

Three of the projects in this book call for some form of quilting. Don't worry—in its most basic form, a quilt is really just two layers of fabric (a pieced top and a backing fabric) with soft material (batting) in between that's been stitched (quilted) through all the layers to keep the batting from shifting around.

Piecing and Patchwork

The geometry of the patchwork in a project like the Frolicking Foxes Lap Quilt on page 38 may make you dizzy, but when you break it down into its steps it's really not that complicated. Start with the right tools (a rotary cutter, a self-healing mat, and clear quilting rulers and squares) and fabrics that inspire you, and the measuring and cutting part of creating patchwork will go much faster.

The actual sewing for patchwork is quite simple, too. Here's the basic process:

1. Take two pieces of fabric and pin one on top of the other with right sides facing.

2. Sew them together (figure 1); generally a ¼-inch (6 mm) seam allowance is used.

figure 1

3. Press the seams open or to one side, usually to the side of the darker fabric (figure 2).

figure 2

Quilt Sandwich

The quilt sandwich is the first step in getting your three quilt layers arranged together. To make one, hold the mayo and simply layer the backing piece (freshly pressed) facedown, then the batting, and then the quilt top (freshly pressed) face up (figure 3). Then, working from the center of the quilt top out toward the edges, secure (or "baste") all three layers together with quilting pins, safety pins, or spray basting adhesive.

quilt top (face up)

batting

backing (face down)

figure 3

Quilting Stitches

The actual stitching known as quilting is, for practical purposes, just a way to keep the layers of the quilt sandwich from shifting around. But the specific quilt stitches you choose can have a big effect on the final look of your quilt. There are many different stitches for both hand and machine quilting, but the following are used in this book:

Stitch in the Ditch: This essentially invisible form of quilting allows the fabrics of your quilt to take center stage. It's a straightforward technique: simply stitch right into the seams of the quilt's patchwork to bind all the layers of your quilt sandwich.

Free-Motion Stitching: If straight lines don't appeal to you, try free-motion quilting by dropping your sewing machine's feed dogs (the teeth under the needle that move the fabric), adding a darning foot (a foot with a small circular opening, sometimes called a free-motion foot), and gently guiding the quilt sandwich through the machine to create a stippling pattern or any other free-form pattern.

Binding

Think of binding as a fabric frame for your quilts. It's seldom anyone's favorite part of a quilting project, but it sure does add that great-looking final touch.

MAKING BINDING STRIPS

To create fabric binding strips, first figure out how many inches of binding you need by adding together the lengths of the four edges you're binding plus 4 to 6 inches (10.2 to 15.2 cm) to be safe. Cut 2½-inch (6.4 cm) wide strips of fabric to this length. You'll probably have to sew a few strips together to get the length needed. When you do, stitch the short ends of the strips together at a 45° angle (figure 4), right sides together. Press the seam open.

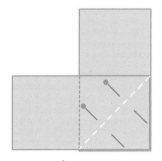

figure 4

Fold your binding strip in half lengthwise and wrong sides together, and press.

ATTACHING THE BINDING

The projects in this book with binding, such as the Noel Wall Hanging on the previous page, call for double fold (or "French") binding.

1. Pin your binding strip (already folded and pressed in half lengthwise, wrong sides together) to the right side of the quilt top, lining up the raw edges.

2. Starting about 5 inches (12.7 cm) from the end of the binding strip, stitch in place using the recommended seam allowance, stopping ¼ inch (6 mm) from the first corner. Backstitch a few times to secure the thread. Clip the thread and remove the quilt from the sewing machine.

3. To miter the corner, fold the binding strip up at 45° toward the top of the quilt (figure 5).

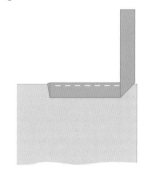

figure 5

4. Fold the strip back down and align it with the next side of the quilt. Begin stitching again (figure 6), ¼ inch (6 mm) in from the folded edge.

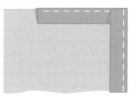

figure 6

5. Continue stitching the binding along the quilt's edge, mitering each corner as you get to it.

6. Stop stitching about 6 inches (15.2 cm) from your starting point. Backstitch. Clip the threads and remove the quilt from the machine. Overlap the ends of the binding strips and trim them down until they overlap by ½ inch (1.3 cm). Stitch them together with right side together. Cut the excess and press the seam open.

7. Stitch down this last section of the binding.

8. Fold the binding to the back of the quilt. Hold it in place (or pin it), and slipstitch (page 21) the binding to the backside of the quilt, mitering the corners as you get to them.

ELF COASTERS

Want to see Santa laugh so his round little belly shakes like a bowl full of jelly?
Set these elf coasters out with his cookies and milk!

PROJECT DESIGNER: MOLLIE JOHANSON

WHAT YOU NEED

(for one coaster)

Embroidery Toolbox (page 9)

Templates (page 124)

White fabric, 5 inches (12.7 cm) square (allows fabric for hooping)

Green or red wool blend felt, 4¼ x 8½ inches (10.8 x 21.6 cm)

Embroidery floss, 1 skein each of red, green, light green, light coral, dark brown, light brown, pink, and light pink*

Double-sided, paper-backed fusible interfacing, 4 inches (10.2 cm) square

Motifs: 228, 229, 230, 231

*Mollie used DMC embroidery floss colors 304, 3346, 3348, 353, 433, 435, 760 and 761.

Finished Size: 4 inches (10.2 cm) diameter

STITCHES

Back Stitch

French Knot

Running Stitch

Satin Stitch

Scallop Stitch

Stem Stitch

x x x x x x x x x x x x x x x x x x x x x x x x

TIP

If you expect to use these coasters with extra hot beverages or on very valuable surfaces, you may wish to add an additional solid circle of felt on the back for more protection.

x x x x x x x x x x x x x x x x x x x x x x x x

INSTRUCTIONS

1. Transfer one elf motif from the CD or page 111 onto the white fabric and embroider according to the stitch guide. See The Eyes Have It on page 14 for special instructions for stitching the eyes.

2. Iron the fusible interfacing to the back of your embroidery, then cut around the design in a circle about 3½ inches (8.9 cm) in diameter.

3. Use the ring template to cut one large solid circle and one ring shape from the felt. Iron the embroidered fabric to the center of the solid felt circle.

4. Place the felt ring on top of the assemblage, then stitch around the outside edge and the inner edge of the felt ring using contrasting floss and the Running Stitch. Hide the knots between the felt layers. Repeat all steps to make the remaining coasters.

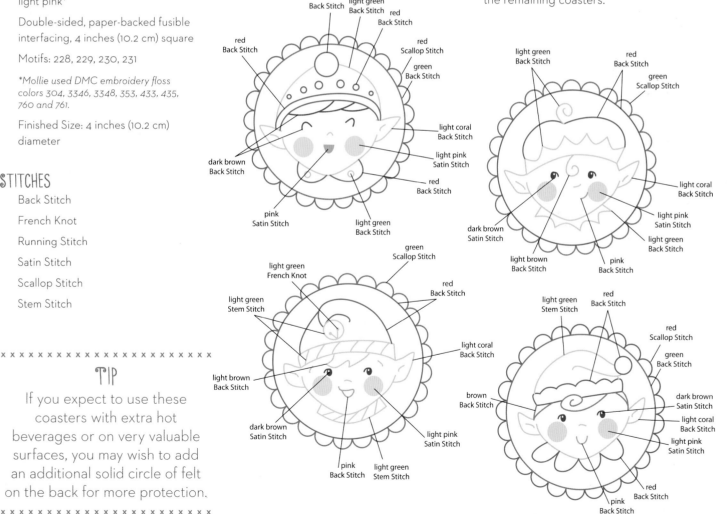

PEACE · JOY · LOVE ADVENT CALENDAR

Move the star from day to day, or tuck a piece of candy or small gift into each pocket of this hand-sewn Advent calendar to count down to Christmas.

PROJECT DESIGNER: AIMEE RAY

WHAT YOU NEED

Embroidery Toolbox (page 9)

Template (page 127)

Aqua felt, 19 x 12 inches (48.3 x 30.5 cm)

Red felt, 12 x 18 inches (30.5 x 45.7 cm)

White felt, 9 x 12 inches (22.9 x 30.5 cm) (or scraps)

Tissue paper

Embroidery floss, 1 skein each of aqua and red, and 2 skeins of white*

Polyester fiberfill stuffing

Wooden dowel rod, ½ inch (1.3 cm) in diameter and 15 inches (28.1 cm) long

2 round wooden dowel caps, 1 inch (2.5 cm) in diameter, with ½ inch (1.3 cm) holes

Wood glue

Aqua grosgrain ribbon, ⅞ inch (2.2 cm) wide and 35 inches (89 cm) long

Motifs: 007, 008, 066, 073, 105

Aimee used DMC embroidery floss colors 598, 321, and white.

Finished Size: 16 x 12 inches (40.6 x 30.5 cm)

STITCHES

Back Stitch

Straight Stitch

INSTRUCTIONS

1. Cut five 9 x 1½-inch (22.9 x 3.8 cm) strips of aqua felt and five matching strips of tissue paper. Trace the number motifs from the CD or on page 94, spacing them evenly, onto the strips of tissue paper. Pin the strips of tissue paper to the strips of felt.

2. Embroider all the numbers and gently remove the tissue paper.

3. Fold 1 inch (2.5 cm) of the top of the red felt rectangle to the back and use the red floss to stitch it with the Stab Stitch (page 22). This will create the slot to slide the dowel into for hanging the banner.

4. Position the felt strips with embroidered numbers onto the red background as shown. Using the Stab Stitch and the aqua floss, sew the strips in place around the sides and bottom of each strip. Remember to leave the top of each strip open. Then sew evenly spaced vertical lines between each number.

5. Trace the lettering, side swirls, and star motifs from the CD or on pages 93, 96, and 98 onto tissue paper and pin

them in place on the red felt. Embroider the motifs according to the stitch guide. When you're finished, gently tear away the tissue paper.

6. Trace the star template onto tissue paper, pin it to white felt, and embroider the motif. Cut it out along with a second, identical shape for the back. Use one thread of white floss to Whip Stitch (page 22) the two pieces together with a little stuffing in between.

7. Slide the dowel into the top of the banner and use wood glue to secure a dowel cap on either end. Tie a bow in the middle of the ribbon and use the Stab Stitch to secure each end of ribbon around either end of the dowel to hang.

Peace ✳ Joy ✳ Love

1 2 3 4 5

6 7 8 9 10

11 12 13 14 15

16 17 18 19 20

21 22 23 24 25

Christmas

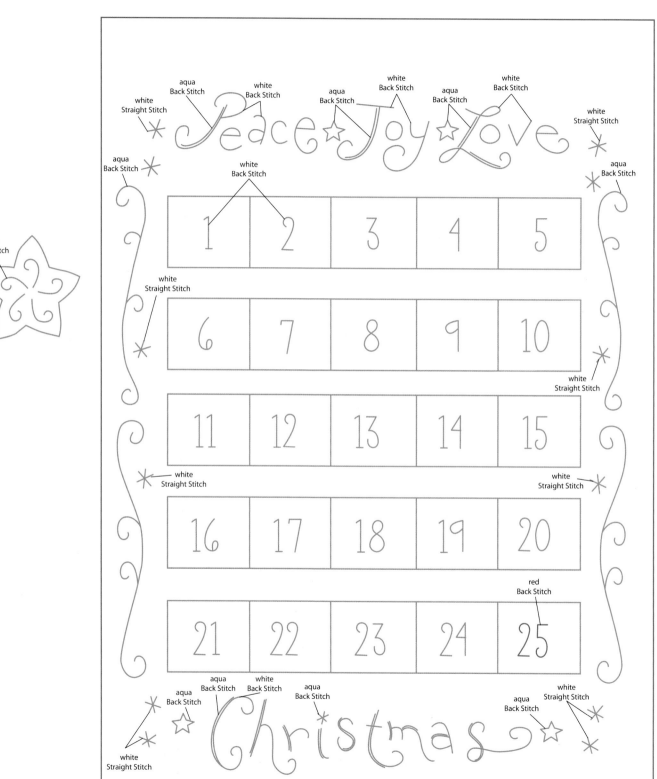

JOLLY HOLIDAYS MINI WREATH

Some of the merriest parts of Christmas are its sweet little details, just like this embroidered wreath. With festive pompoms and an array of cheerful colors, Carina's wreath will brighten up any space.

PROJECT DESIGNER: CARINA ENVOLDSEN-HARRIS

WHAT YOU NEED

Embroidery Toolbox (page 9)

White cotton fabric, two 8-inch (20.3 cm) squares

Embroidery floss, 1 skein each of light pink, pink, orange, light green, green, dark green, jade, red, and dark red*

White fusible interfacing, two 8-inch (20.3 cm) squares

White mini pompom fringe, 20 inches (50.8 cm) in length

Motif: 176

*Carina used DMC embroidery floss colors 3708, 956, 721, 3348, 907, 905, 3851, 666, and 304.

Finished Size: 7¼ inches (18.4 cm) square

STITCHES

Back Stitch

Fly Stitch

Satin Stitch

INSTRUCTIONS

1. Transfer the wreath motif from the CD or page 105 to the center front of one piece of the white cotton and embroider according to the stitch guide.

2. Iron the interfacing to the wrong side of both pieces of white cotton.

3. Cut the white mini pompom fringe into one 12-inch (30.5 cm) and one 8-inch (20.3 cm) length.

4. Place the unembroidered piece of cotton/interfacing on a flat surface, cotton side up. Using figure 1 for reference, pin the shorter piece of fringe along the bottom edge, with the pompoms facing in. Pin the longer piece of pompom fringe at the two points at the top, about 1¾ inches (4.4 cm) in from each side. Make sure the fringe is arranged as shown.

5. Place the embroidered cotton/interfacing piece on top, embroidered side down, making sure the design is oriented correctly: the poinsettia with the bow should be at the bottom. Mark a 3¾-inch (9.5 cm) turning-gap opening at the top between the two fringe ends. Pin all the edges together.

6. Sew around the outside edge with a ¼-inch (6 mm) seam allowance, leaving the turning gap open.

7. Clip the corners and turn the assemblage inside out.

8. Slipstitch the turning gap closed.

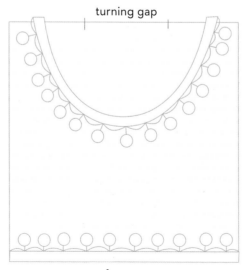

turning gap

figure 1

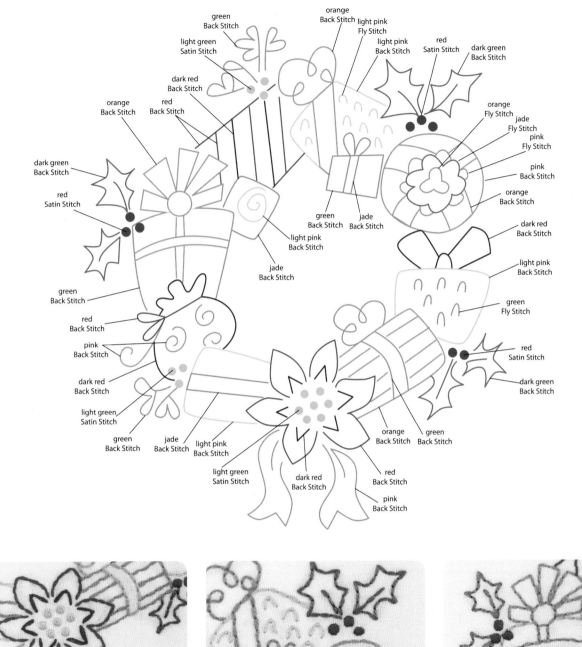

green
Back Stitch

light green
Satin Stitch

orange
Back Stitch

light pink
Fly Stitch

light pink
Back Stitch

red
Satin Stitch

dark green
Back Stitch

dark red
Back Stitch

red
Back Stitch

orange
Back Stitch

orange
Fly Stitch

jade
Fly Stitch

pink
Fly Stitch

pink
Back Stitch

dark green
Back Stitch

red
Satin Stitch

orange
Back Stitch

green
Back Stitch

jade
Back Stitch

light pink
Back Stitch

jade
Back Stitch

dark red
Back Stitch

light pink
Back Stitch

green
Fly Stitch

green
Back Stitch

red
Back Stitch

pink
Back Stitch

dark red
Back Stitch

light green
Satin Stitch

green
Back Stitch

jade
Back Stitch

light pink
Back Stitch

red
Satin Stitch

dark green
Back Stitch

light green
Satin Stitch

dark red
Back Stitch

orange
Back Stitch

green
Back Stitch

red
Back Stitch

pink
Back Stitch

PENGUIN STOCKING ORNAMENTS

Stitch up this mix-and-match set of miniature stockings
to hang on your tree or from a garland.

PROJECT DESIGNER: LAURA HOWARD

WHAT YOU NEED

Embroidery Toolbox (page 9)

Template (page 124)

Pale blue felt, two 9 x 12-inch (22.9 x 30.5 cm) sheets

Light blue felt, two 9 x 12-inch (22.9 x 30.5 cm) sheets

Medium blue felt, two 9 x 12-inch (22.9 x 30.5 cm) sheets

Tissue paper

Embroidery floss, 1 skein each of blue, orange, black, light green, green, and white*

Pinking shears

Narrow ribbon, three shades of blue to match felt colors

Sewing thread, three shades of blue to match felt colors

Silver or blue sequins

Silver or blue seed beads

Narrow ribbon, three shades of blue to match felt colors

Motifs: 147, 148, 149

*Laura used DMC embroidery floss colors 796, 741, 310, 907, 905, and white.

Finished Size: 4 inches (10.2 cm) long

STITCHES

Back Stitch

Running Stitch

Satin Stitch

Straight Stitch

Whip Stitch

INSTRUCTIONS

For the Penguin Stockings

1. Trace one penguin motif from the CD or page 102 onto a piece of tissue paper and cut it out roughly. Hoop a sheet of blue felt, and pin the traced penguin motif in the center.

2. Embroider the penguin motif according to the stitch guide. Back Stitch along the lines and around the eyes.

3. Carefully tear away the tissue paper to reveal your stitched motif. Use tweezers or your needle to remove any small or fiddly pieces. Then use more black embroidery floss to fill in the centers of the eyes. Remove the felt from the hoop.

4. Trace the stocking template onto a piece of tissue paper and cut it out. Position the stocking shape over the embroidered penguin so your stitching isn't too close to the edges of the stocking. Pin the template in place and cut out the felt stocking shape. Then use the template to cut out a second stocking shape in matching blue felt.

5. Use pinking shears to cut a strip from one of the other shades of blue felt. The strip should be approximately ½ inch (1.3 cm) wide and slightly longer than the top of the stocking. Pin this strip to the front stocking piece, leaving a small gap at the top. Sew it in place with two lines of Running Stitch in the matching sewing thread. Then remove the pins and trim away the excess felt overhanging the sides of the stocking.

6. Embellish the top strip using a white-and-silver color scheme or mixed-and-matched blues to coordinate with the blue felt. Use three threads of the white floss to sew two rows of Back Stitch, a line of zigzag stitching, or a row of sequins (sew each sequin in place with two horizontal stitches).

7. To decorate the stocking body, fill the felt around the penguin with randomly spaced embellishments. Add sequins (using three stitches of matching sewing thread per sequin) or seed beads (using a double thickness of sewing thread to match the felt), or embroider stars (using three threads of the white floss and sewing four overlapping stitches to create a star shape).

8. Cut a 5-inch (12.7 cm) length of narrow ribbon in a shade of blue that matches the stocking. Fold the ribbon into a loop and position it near the straight edge of the back stocking piece. The ribbon ends should overlap the felt by about

½ inch (1.3 cm). Sew the loop in place with Whip Stitches and matching sewing thread, sewing into the felt but not through it.

9. Attach the front and back of the stocking using the Whip Stitch in matching sewing thread around the edges. Either sew all the way around the stocking, or leave the top edge open.

For the Plain Stockings

1. Use the stocking template to cut out two stocking shapes from matching blue felt.

2. Add a pinked strip of felt to the top of the front stocking shape, as in steps 5 and 6 for the penguin stockings.

3. Decorate the stocking as in step 7 for the penguin stockings, covering the whole front stocking shape with embellishments.

4. Follow steps 8 and 9 for the penguin stockings to add a ribbon loop and sew the front and back of the stocking together.

x x x x x x x x x x x x x x x x x x x x x x

TIP
If you want to leave your stockings open so you can put small treats such as candy canes inside, keep the back of your stitching as neat as possible and avoid carrying threads across the back of your work.

x x x x x x x x x x x x x x x x x x x x x x

FROLICKING FOXES LAP QUILT

Playful foxes and a fresh take on holiday colors
make this lap quilt merry and bright.

PROJECT DESIGNER: JOHN Q. ADAMS
(EMBROIDERED BY AIMEE RAY, MACHINE-QUILTED BY JENNY SCHEIDT)

WHAT YOU NEED

Embroidery Toolbox (page 9)

Sturdy white quilter's cotton, 1⅔ yards (1.5 m)

Orange fabric, ½ yard (45.7 cm)

24 squares of assorted printed fabric, 10 inches (25.4 cm) square each

Binding fabric, ⅔ yard (61 cm)

Batting, 56 x 72 inches (142 x 183 cm)

Backing fabric, 4 yards (3.7 m)

Embroidery floss, 1 skein each of green, light green, brown, orange, light orange, red orange, and yellow*

Rotary cutter

Cutting mat

Quilting ruler

Motifs: 130, 131, 132, 133, 134, 135

*Aimee used DMC embroidery floss colors 470, 472, 433, 3853, 3854, 720, and 3855.

Finished size: 48 x 64 inches (122 x 162.5 cm)

STITCHES

Satin Stitch

Split Stitch

Straight Stitch

INSTRUCTIONS

Note: Quilting Essentials can be found starting on page 23.

Cutting the Pieces

1. From the white quilter's cotton, cut:
   • 6 squares, 14½ inches (36.8 cm) square each
   • 12 strips, 2½ x 12½ inches (6.4 x 31.8 cm) each
   • 12 strips, 2½ x 16½ inches (6.4 x 41.9 cm) each

2. From the orange framing fabric, cut:
   • 12 strips, 2½ x 8½ inches (6.4 x 21.6 cm) each
   • 12 strips, 2½ x 12½ inches (6.4 x 31.8 cm) each

Assembling the Blocks

Block A (Embroidery Blocks)

1. Transfer the fox motifs from the CD or page 101 to the six 14½-inch (36.8 cm) squares of white quilter's cotton. Embroider the motifs according to the stitch guide.

2. Trim each embroidered block down to 8½ inches (21.6 cm) square, making sure the embroidered motif is centered in each block.

3. Sew one of the 2½ x 8½-inch (6.4 x 21.6 cm) orange strips to the left and right side of each embroidered square. Press the seams outward toward the orange fabric.

4. Sew one of the 2½ x 12½-inch (6.4 x 31.8 cm) orange strips to the top and the bottom of each embroidered square. Press the seams outward toward the orange fabric.

5. Sew one of the 2½ x 12½-inch (6.4 x 31.8 cm) white quilter's cotton strips to the left and right side of each orange frame. Press the seams outward toward the orange fabric.

6. Sew one of the 2½ x 16½-inch (6.4 x 41.9 cm) white quilter's cotton strips to the top and the bottom of each orange frame. Press the seams outward toward the orange fabric. The block should now measure 16½ inches (41.9 cm) square.

Block B (Hourglass Blocks)

1. Select two of the 10-inch (25.4 cm) print squares. Mark a diagonal line on the wrong side of one of the squares (figure 1).

2. Align the two squares with right sides together. Sew a seam on either side of the line with a ¼-inch (6 mm) seam allowance (figure 2).

3. With the rotary cutter, cut the block along the marked line (figure 3). Open and press the seams to the darker fabric to create two half-square triangles (HSTs).

4. Repeat steps 1 through 3 with the remaining 22 print squares to create a totoal of 48 HSTs.

5. Select two HSTs (figure 4). Match the HSTs, making sure the seams are aligned. Draw a diagonal line on the wrong side of the top HSTs in the opposite direction from the existing seam. Sew a seam on either side of the marked line, using a ¼-inch (6 mm) seam allowance.

figure 1

figure 2

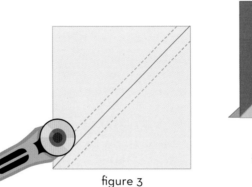

figure 3

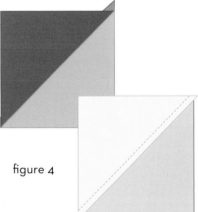

figure 4

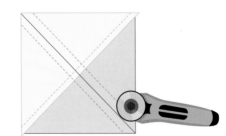

figure 5

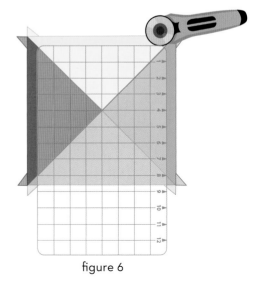

figure 6

6. With the rotary cutter, cut the block along the marked line (figure 5). Press the seams open to create two hourglass blocks.

7. Trim each block to 8½ inches (21.6 cm) square. Use a quilting ruler to do so, making sure to match the diagonal line on the ruler to the diagonal seam on the block (figure 6).

8. Repeat steps 5 through 7 to create 24 hourglass blocks. Make sure all blocks are trimmed to 8½ inches (21.6 cm) square.

9. Each Block B is comprised of four hourglass blocks, sewn together in a 2 x 2 format. Select four hourglass blocks for each Block B and determine a pleasing layout for the blocks. Sew one pair of hourglass blocks together and then the other pair. The finished block should measure 16½ inches (41.9 cm) square.

Assembling the Quilt Top

1. Lay the embroidered and pieced quilt blocks out in a 3 x 4 grid in an eye-pleasing arrangement, alternating between embroidered blocks (Block A) and pieced blocks (Block B).

2. Sew each row together, pressing seams toward the embroidered blocks.

3. Join the rows to complete the quilt top.

Making the Backing Piece

1. Cut the 4-yard (3.7 m) backing fabric piece into two 2-yard (1.8 m) pieces. Trim all selvages. Pin and stitch these two pieces together along the long 2-yard (1.8 m) edge. Press the seam open. This should result in a backing piece measuring approximately 84 x 72 inches (213.4 x 182.8 cm). Trim the sides to approximately 56 x 72 inches (142.2 x 182.8 cm).

Finishing the Quilt

1. Make a "quilt sandwich" (page 23) by layering the backing piece (right side down), the batting, and then the quilt top (right side up) to prepare for quilting.

2. Baste or pin, and then quilt as desired (page 24). The project shown was quilted with free-motion quilting. Trim any excess batting or backing fabric.

3. Stitch the binding strips together end-to-end to make one long strip and bind the quilt (page 25).

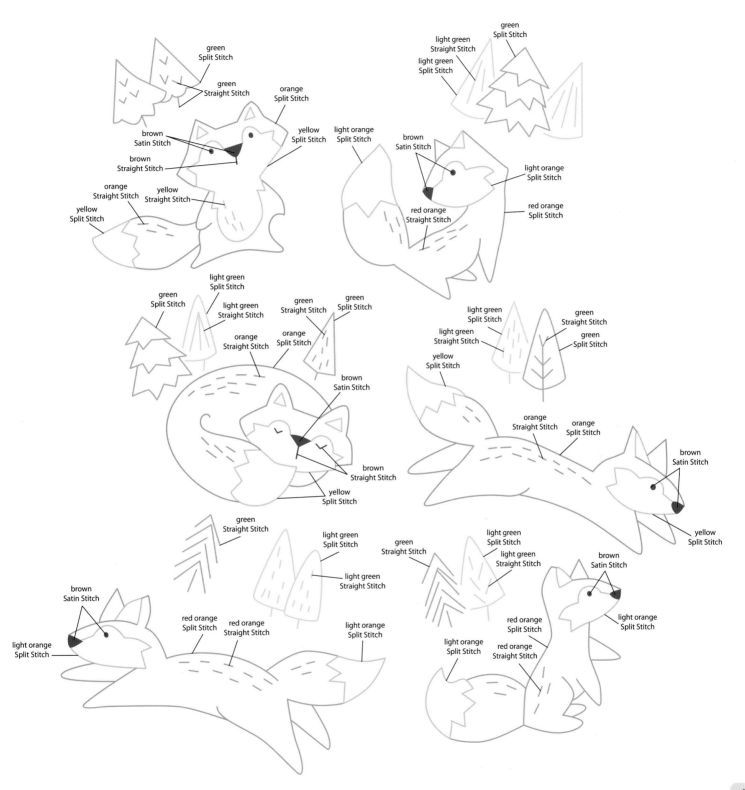

green
Split Stitch

green
Straight Stitch

orange
Split Stitch

yellow
Split Stitch

brown
Satin Stitch

brown
Straight Stitch

orange
Straight Stitch

yellow
Straight Stitch

yellow
Split Stitch

light green
Straight Stitch

green
Split Stitch

light green
Split Stitch

brown
Satin Stitch

light orange
Split Stitch

light orange
Split Stitch

red orange
Straight Stitch

red orange
Split Stitch

light green
Split Stitch

green
Split Stitch

light green
Straight Stitch

green
Straight Stitch

orange
Straight Stitch

orange
Split Stitch

green
Split Stitch

brown
Satin Stitch

brown
Straight Stitch

yellow
Split Stitch

light green
Split Stitch

light green
Straight Stitch

green
Straight Stitch

green
Split Stitch

yellow
Split Stitch

orange
Straight Stitch

orange
Split Stitch

brown
Satin Stitch

yellow
Split Stitch

green
Straight Stitch

light green
Split Stitch

light green
Straight Stitch

green
Straight Stitch

light green
Split Stitch

light green
Straight Stitch

brown
Satin Stitch

brown
Satin Stitch

red orange
Split Stitch

red orange
Straight Stitch

light orange
Split Stitch

light orange
Split Stitch

light orange
Split Stitch

red orange
Split Stitch

red orange
Straight Stitch

light orange
Split Stitch

SOFT NATIVITY

These sweet freestanding nativity figures are
sure to become a Christmas heirloom.

PROJECT DESIGNER: AIMEE RAY

WHAT YOU NEED

Embroidery Toolbox (page 9)

Templates (page 128)

½ yard (45.7 cm) white linen

Cream felt, 9 x 12 inches (22.9 x 30.5 cm)

Embroidery floss, 1 skein each of aqua, brown, dark brown, light brown, green, light green, peach, pink, dark pink, red, and ecru*

Small funnel for filling the figures

Plastic beanbag pellets, dry rice, or beans (small amount for weighting the figures)

Polyester fiberfill stuffing

Motifs: 146, 151, 216, 218, 220, 221, 222

Aimee used DMC embroidery floss colors 3811, 435, 3862, 422, 471, 472, 950, 761, 760, 3328, and ecru.

Finished Size: 1¾ to 4¼ inches (4.4 to 10.8 cm) tall

STITCHES

Back Stitch

French Knot

Lazy Daisy

Satin Stitch

Scallop Stitch

Split Stitch

Straight Stitch

INSTRUCTIONS

1. Transfer the motifs from the CD or pages 102 and 110 to the linen, leaving at least 1 inch (2.5 cm) of space around the outside of each figure. Embroider the motifs according to the stitch guides.

2. Using the outline templates as guides, cut out each figure, leaving ½ inch (1.3 cm) of extra fabric around the edge. Cut another piece of linen the same size for each figure. Trace the bottom pieces onto the felt and cut them out.

3. Pin the front and back pieces together with right sides facing. For each figure, begin by sewing up from either bottom edge, leaving the bottom open as well as a 1-inch (2.5 cm) space open on one side. Next, spread the bottom open into an oval and pin the felt piece in place at the bottom of each figure. Sew it in place.

4. Trim and notch the edges and turn each figure right side out. Using a funnel, fill the bottom of each figure with ½ inch (1.3 cm) of pellets, dry rice, or dry beans. Fill the rest of the figure firmly with the stuffing.

5. Stitch up the hole using the Hidden Stitch (page 21).

215   217   219   150

You can add Three Wise Men and a camel to your Nativity, too: pages 102 and 110.

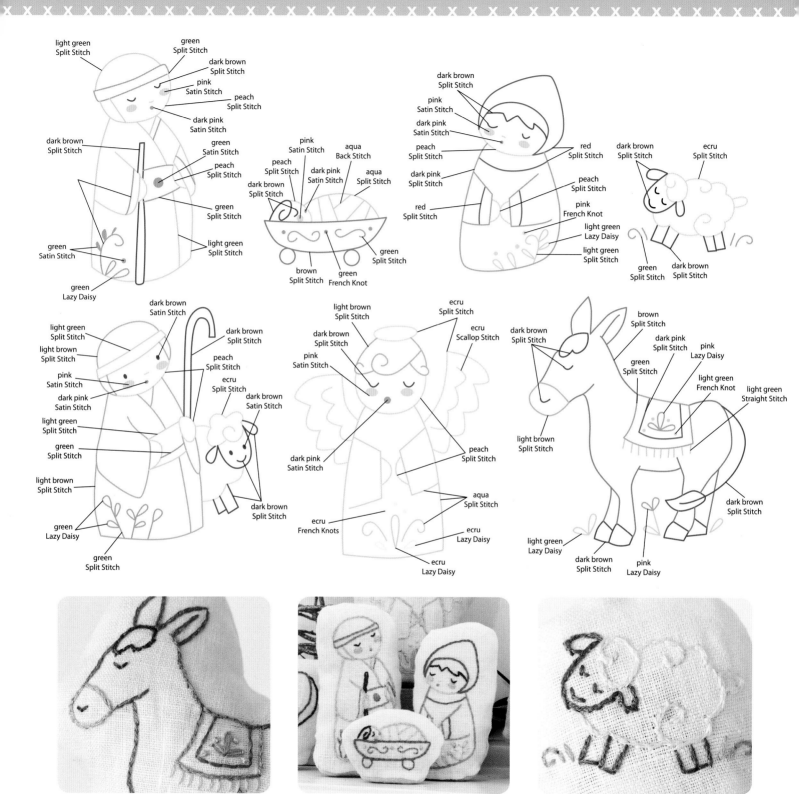

light green
Split Stitch

green
Split Stitch

dark brown
Split Stitch

pink
Satin Stitch

peach
Split Stitch

dark pink
Satin Stitch

dark brown
Split Stitch

green
Satin Stitch

peach
Split Stitch

green
Split Stitch

green
Satin Stitch

light green
Split Stitch

green
Lazy Daisy

pink
Satin Stitch

aqua
Back Stitch

peach
Split Stitch

dark pink
Satin Stitch

aqua
Split Stitch

dark brown
Split Stitch

brown
Split Stitch

green
French Knot

green
Split Stitch

dark brown
Split Stitch

pink
Satin Stitch

dark pink
Satin Stitch

peach
Split Stitch

dark pink
Split Stitch

red
Split Stitch

red
Split Stitch

peach
Split Stitch

pink
French Knot

light green
Lazy Daisy

light green
Split Stitch

green
Split Stitch

dark brown
Split Stitch

dark brown
Split Stitch

ecru
Split Stitch

dark brown
Satin Stitch

dark brown
Split Stitch

light green
Split Stitch

light brown
Split Stitch

pink
Satin Stitch

dark pink
Satin Stitch

peach
Split Stitch

ecru
Split Stitch

dark brown
Satin Stitch

light green
Split Stitch

green
Split Stitch

light brown
Split Stitch

dark brown
Split Stitch

green
Lazy Daisy

green
Split Stitch

light brown
Split Stitch

dark brown
Split Stitch

ecru
Split Stitch

ecru
Scallop Stitch

pink
Satin Stitch

dark pink
Satin Stitch

peach
Split Stitch

aqua
Split Stitch

ecru
French Knots

ecru
Lazy Daisy

ecru
Lazy Daisy

dark brown
Split Stitch

brown
Split Stitch

dark pink
Split Stitch

green
Split Stitch

pink
Lazy Daisy

light green
French Knot

light green
Straight Stitch

light brown
Split Stitch

dark brown
Split Stitch

light green
Lazy Daisy

dark brown
Split Stitch

pink
Lazy Daisy

WINTER WONDERLAND STOCKING

Stitch these sledding woodland critters on a stocking cuff
for a fun surprise on Christmas morning.

PROJECT DESIGNER: MOLLIE JOHANSON

WHAT YOU NEED

Embroidery Toolbox (page 9)

Templates (page 126)

White wool-blend felt, one 9 x 12-inch (22.9 x 30.5 cm) sheet

Light green wool blend felt, two 12 x 18-inch (30.5 x 45.7 cm) sheets

Tissue paper

Embroidery floss, 1 skein each of green, aqua, pink, dark brown, brown, light brown, and ecru*

Motif: 121

Mollie used DMC embroidery floss in colors 3346, 598, 433, 434, 437, 352, and ecru.

Finished Size: 15 inches (38.1 cm) long

STITCHES

Back Stitch

Fly Stitch

French Knot

Satin Stitch

Straight Stitch

INSTRUCTIONS

1. Use the templates to cut one heel and one toe piece from the white felt. Then cut two 9 x 4½-inch (22.9 x 11.4 cm) cuff pieces from the white felt. Use the template to cut two stocking pieces and one 1 x 7-inch (2.5 x 17.8 cm) hanger piece from the light green felt.

2. Trace the motif from the CD or page 99 onto tissue paper, and then pin the tissue paper to one cuff piece, centering the design. Stitch the motif through the paper and felt, according to the stitch guide. Use three threads for the eyes, noses, mouths, and foot pads, and six threads for everything else. See page 14 for special instructions for stitching the eyes. When done, gently tear away the tissue paper, and use tweezers or your needle to remove any stuck bits of paper.

3. Using the photo for reference, place the white heel and toe pieces on the front stocking piece and stitch around each piece with six threads of light green floss and the Running Stitch.

4. Pin the front and back stocking pieces with wrong sides together and stitch around the shape with six threads of light green floss and the Running Stitch, leaving the top open.

5. Pin the embroidered cuff to the front of the stocking so that the top edges are aligned. Stitch along the top edge with six threads of light green floss and the Running Stitch. Repeat with the second cuff piece on the back.

6. Stitch the sides of the cuff pieces together with the Running Stitch, and add a line of decorative running stitch to the bottom edge of each cuff piece.

7. Fold the hanger strip in half so it measures 1 x 3½ inches (2.5 x 8.9 cm), and position it between the layers on the top right inside of the stocking. Stitch the hanger in place with the Running Stitch, catching only the green felt (not the cuff) to hide the stitches between the layers.

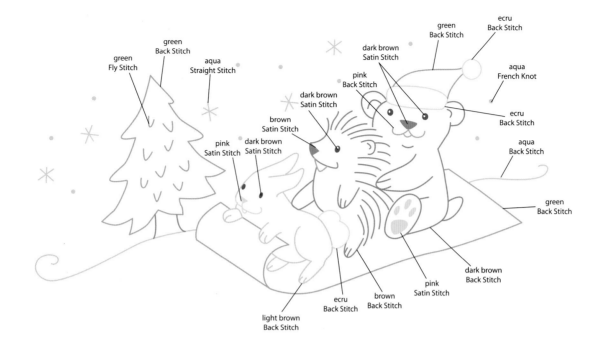

green
Fly Stitch

green
Back Stitch

aqua
Straight Stitch

green
Back Stitch

ecru
Back Stitch

dark brown
Satin Stitch

pink
Back Stitch

aqua
French Knot

dark brown
Satin Stitch

ecru
Back Stitch

brown
Satin Stitch

pink
Satin Stitch

dark brown
Satin Stitch

aqua
Back Stitch

green
Back Stitch

dark brown
Back Stitch

light brown
Back Stitch

ecru
Back Stitch

brown
Back Stitch

pink
Satin Stitch

FELT STAR TREE TOPPER

Hang a shining star upon the highest bough!

PROJECT DESIGNER: AIMEE RAY

WHAT YOU NEED

Embroidery Toolbox (page 9)

Templates (page 127)

Cream felt, two 9 x 12-inch (22.9 x 30.5 cm) sheets

White felt, one 9 x 12-inch (22.9 x 30.5 cm) sheet (or scraps)

Embroidery floss, 1 skein each of metallic silver and metallic gold*

*Aimee used DMC Precious Metal Effects embroidery floss colors E168 and E3821.

Finished Size: 7 inches (17.8 cm) wide

STITCHES

Blanket Stitch

Lazy Daisy

Running Stitch

Satin Stitch

Straight Stitch

x x x x x x x x x x x x x x

TIP

This central star design is pretty easy to stitch free-hand, but you can also find a motif on page 98.

x x x x x x x x x x x x x x

INSTRUCTIONS

1. Using the large star template, cut two stars from the cream felt, and five triangles and one small star from white felt.

2. Position the white pieces as shown onto one of the cream stars and stitch them in place using the floss and the stitches indicated in the stitch guide.

3. Embroider the rest of the star according to the stitch guide.

4. Pin the two star pieces wrong sides together. Blanket Stitch the stars together at the outer edges, beginning at one of the bottom star points and stitching all around the top of the star. When you reach the other bottom point, continue the Blanket Stitch only on the front piece of felt, leaving the bottom of the star open to slide over the topmost branch of your Christmas tree.

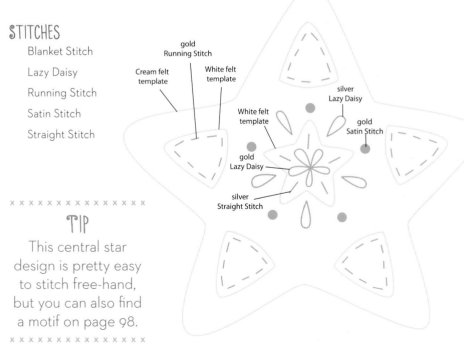

gold Running Stitch

White felt template

Cream felt template

White felt template

silver Lazy Daisy

gold Satin Stitch

gold Lazy Daisy

silver Straight Stitch

VARIATION

Try this star in red and pink for a fun, colorful tree topper!

AUTUMN TO WINTER PLACEMATS

These placemats are versatile enough to use from early
autumn straight through the holidays!

PROJECT DESIGNER: AIMEE RAY

WHAT YOU NEED

Embroidery Toolbox (page 9)

Green quilter's cotton fabric, ½ yard (45.7 cm) for each 12 x 16-inch (30.5 x 40.6 cm) placemat

Embroidery floss, 1 skein each of aqua, light brown, brown, and green*

Green sewing thread

Motifs: 174, 326

*Aimee used DMC embroidery floss in colors 598, 435, 434, and 471.

Finished Size: 12 x 16 inches (30.5 x 40.6 cm)

STITCHES

Back Stitch

Satin Stitch

Running Stitch

Scallop Stitch

Straight Stitch

INSTRUCTIONS

1. For each placemat, cut two 13 x 17-inch (33 x 43.2 cm) rectangles from the fabric, one for the front and one for the back of each placemat.

2. Transfer the pinecone or acorn motif from the CD or pages 105 and 122 to the bottom right corner of each front piece, then embroider the motif according to the stitch guide.

3. Pin the two pieces of fabric right sides together and, with the green sewing thread, stitch ½ inch (1.3 cm) in from the edge, leaving a 2-inch (5.1 cm) opening. Trim the corners and turn the placemat right side out through the opening. Push out the corners and press the seams flat.

4. Topstitch (page 21) the placemat ¼ inch (6 mm) in from the edge on all sides using all six threads of the green floss and the Running Stitch.

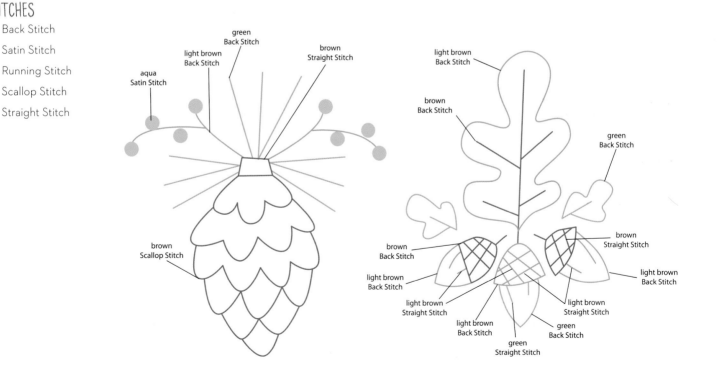

PRANCER PILLOW

Pour yourself a mug of hot cocoa and cozy up with this pretty pillow, or skip the cocoa and sink blissfully into its lovely softness for a long winter's nap.

PROJECT DESIGNER: JOHN Q. ADAMS
(EMBROIDERED BY AIMEE RAY)

WHAT YOU NEED

Embroidery Toolbox (page 9)

White quilter's cotton, 16 inches (40.6 cm) square

Scraps of 11 different print fabrics

1 piece of muslin or scrap fabric for backing the quilted strips, 24 x 34 inches (61 x 86.3 cm)

2 pieces of fabric for pillow back, 16½ x 32 inches (41.9 x 81.2 cm) each

Embroidery floss, 1 skein each of green, light green, pink, red, aqua, light brown, brown, and dark brown*

1 piece of batting, 20 x 30 inches (50.8 x 76.2 cm)

Rotary cutter

Cutting mat

Quilting ruler

Pillow form, 16 x 26 inches (40.6 x 66 cm)

Motif: 129

*Aimee used DMC embroidery floss colors 905, 906, 3712, 321, 598, 437, 435, and 433.

Finished Size: 16 x 26 inches (40.6 x 66 cm)

STITCHES

Back Stitch

Satin Stitch

Split Stitch

Straight Stitch

INSTRUCTIONS

Note: Quilting Essentials can be found starting on page 23.

Embroidery

Transfer the reindeer motif from the CD or page 100 to the center of the square of white quilter's cotton. Embroider according to the stitch guide. When complete, trim the embroidered block down to 12½ inches (31.8 cm) square.

Pillow Top Assembly

1. Referencing page 56, cut the following pieces from the fabrics:
- Fabric A: two 1½ x 7½-inch (3.8 x 19 cm) strips, one 1½ x 12½-inch (3.8 x 31.8 cm) strip
- Fabric B: two 2½ x 7½-inch (6.4 x 19 cm) strips, one 1½ x 12½-inch (3.8 x 31.8 cm) strip
- Fabric C: two 1½ x 7½-inch (3.8 x 19 cm) strips
- Fabric D: two 2½ x 7½-inch (6.4 x 19 cm) strips
- Fabric E: two 1½ x 7½-inch (3.8 x 19 cm) strips
- Fabric F: two 2½ x 7½-inch (6.4 x 19 cm) strips
- Fabric G: two 1½ x 7½-inch (3.8 x 19 cm) strips
- Fabric H: two 2½ x 7½-inch (6.4 x 19 cm) strips
- Fabric I: two 1½ x 7½-inch (3.8 x 19 cm) strips
- Fabric J: two 2½ x 7½-inch (6.4 x 19 cm) strips, one 1½ x 12½-inch (3.8 x 31.8 cm) strip
- Fabric K: two 1½ x 7½-inch (3.8 x 19 cm) strips, one 1½ x 12½-inch (3.8 x 31.8 cm) strip

A B C D E F G H I J K

figure 1

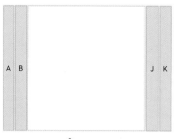

A B J K

figure 2

2. Using the figure 1 for reference, piece together 11 of the 7½-inch (19 cm) strips in order from left to right (A to K) along their 7½-inch (19 cm) edges. Press the seams open.

3. Repeat step 2 with the remaining 11 of the 7½-inch (19 cm) strips, creating a second identical strip set.

4. You should have four strips remaining, all measuring 1½ x 12½ inches (3.8 x 31.8 cm) (fabrics A, B, J, and K.) Using figure 2 for reference, piece together the middle panel of the pillow.

5. Assemble the three pieces of the pillow top by sewing the strip sets together along their 16½-inch (41.9 cm) edges as shown in figure 3.

6. Layer the pillow top, batting, and piece of scrap fabric into a "quilt sandwich" (page 23) to prepare for quilting. Baste and quilt. The project shown was quilted using Stitch in the Ditch (page 24) in all sewn seams.

7. Trim the pillow top to 16½ x 26½ inches (41.9 x 67.3cm).

Assemble the Pillow Cover

1. To make the envelope-fold back for the pillow, first fold each of the two backing pieces in half along their 32-inch (81.2 cm) side, wrong sides together, so you end up with two pieces each measuring 16 x 16½ inches (40.6 x 41.9 cm). Press the creases well to create crisp folds. These pieces will be used to create an envelope back for the pillow.

2. Stack the pillow components in the following order:
- Quilted pillow top, face up.
- Top half of the envelope back, aligning raw edges to the top, left, and right sides of the pillow top. The fold should span across the middle of the pillow top.
- Bottom half of envelope back, aligning raw edges to the bottom, left, and right sides of the pillow top. The fold should span across the middle of the pillow top, overlapping the top half of the backing.

3. Pin around all four sides of the pillow.

4. Sew a seam around all four sides of the pillow with a ¼-inch (6 mm) seam allowance. For added strength (useful when inserting the pillow form), go around twice.

5. Turn the pillowcase inside out through the envelope back. Insert the pillow form and enjoy!

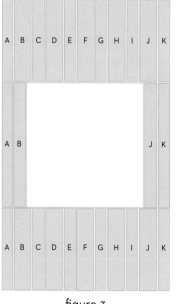

A B C D E F G H I J K

A B J K

A B C D E F G H I J K

figure 3

TIP

This pillow looks great with
a horizontal orientation, too.
Just turn the embroidered
piece 90° before attaching
it to the pieced fabric.

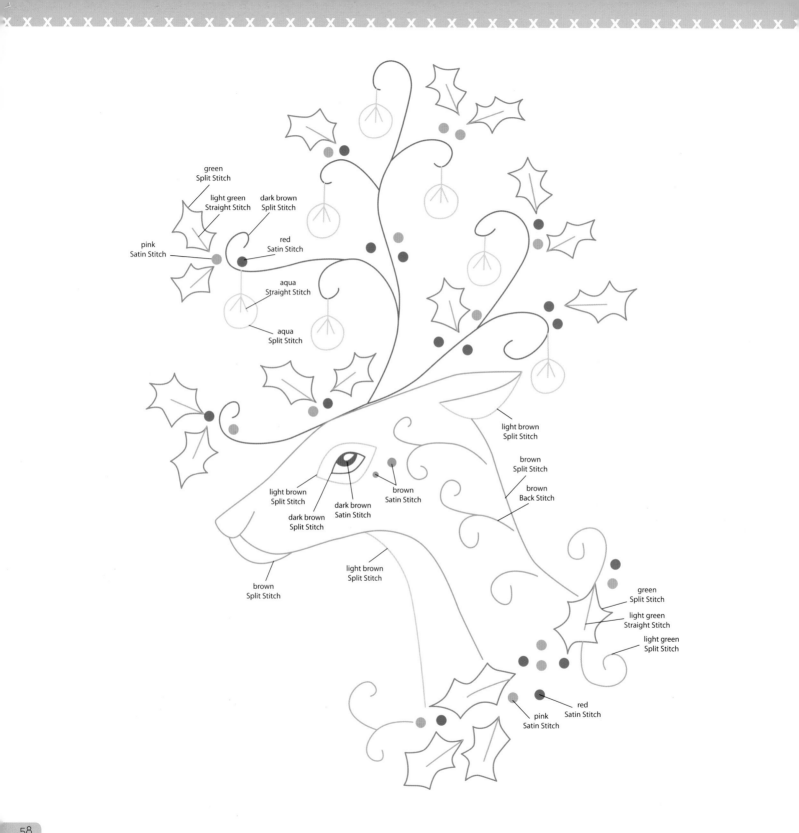

green
Split Stitch

light green
Straight Stitch

dark brown
Split Stitch

pink
Satin Stitch

red
Satin Stitch

aqua
Straight Stitch

aqua
Split Stitch

light brown
Split Stitch

brown
Split Stitch

brown
Back Stitch

light brown
Split Stitch

brown
Satin Stitch

dark brown
Satin Stitch

dark brown
Split Stitch

brown
Split Stitch

light brown
Split Stitch

green
Split Stitch

light green
Straight Stitch

light green
Split Stitch

red
Satin Stitch

pink
Satin Stitch

SLEEPY MOUSE PILLOWCASE

Not a creature was stirring, not even a mouse!

PROJECT DESIGNER: MOLLIE JOHANSON

WHAT YOU NEED

Embroidery Toolbox (page 9)

White cotton fabric: ⅓ yard (.4 m)

Print cotton fabric: ¾ yard (.7 m)

Embroidery floss, 1 skein each of red, turquoise, aqua, brown, dark brown, pink, and white*

White sewing thread

Motifs: 006, 127

Mollie used DMC embroidery floss in colors 321, 597, 598, 435, 433, 761, and white.

Finished Size: 30 x 21 inches (76.2 x 53.3 cm)

STITCHES

Back Stitch

Chain Stitch

French Knot

Running Stitch

Satin Stitch

Stem Stitch

Straight Stitch

INSTRUCTIONS

1. Transfer the motifs from the CD or pages 93 and 100 (text and mouse) onto the white fabric, positioned in the upper left area of the fabric, about 3 inches (7.6 cm) in from the left edge and 1½ inches (3.8 cm) from the top. Embroider the motifs according to the stitch guide, using three strands of floss throughout the entire motif (see figure 1).

2. Cut the embroidered white fabric to 11 x 44 inches (27.9 x 111.7 cm), and cut the print fabric to 26 x 44 inches (66 x 111.7 cm).

3. Fold the white fabric in half lengthwise with wrong sides facing, then pin the raw edge of this cuff to the long side of the print fabric, with the embroidered side facing the right side of the print fabric. Sew the pieces together, using a ¼-inch (6 mm) seam allowance (see figure 2). Fold the cuff up and press the seam toward the print fabric.

4. Fold the pillowcase in half with right sides together, making sure that the folded edge and seam of the cuff match. Pin the open side and bottom, then sew (see figure 3). Turn right side out.

5. Use three threads of the aqua floss to add lines of Running Stitch near the seam and folded edge of the cuff, catching only the top layer of fabric.

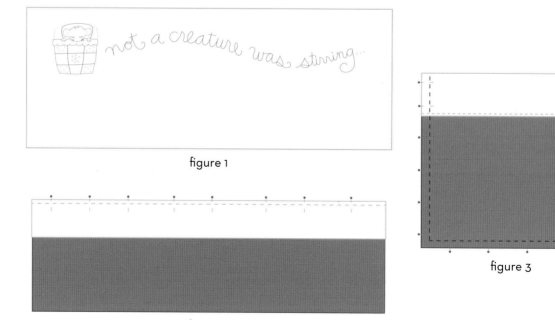

figure 1

figure 2

figure 3

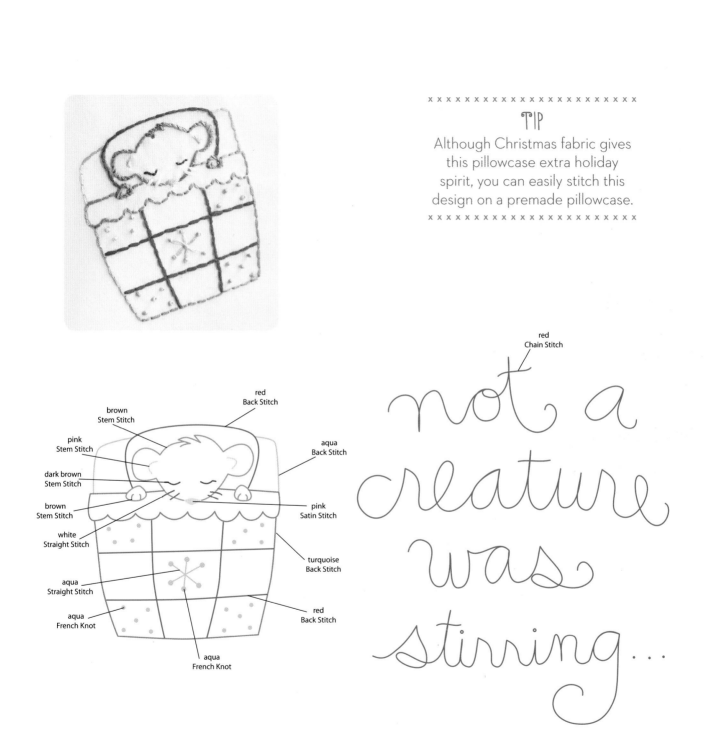

TIP
Although Christmas fabric gives this pillowcase extra holiday spirit, you can easily stitch this design on a premade pillowcase.

red
Chain Stitch

not a creature was stirring...

red
Back Stitch

brown
Stem Stitch

pink
Stem Stitch

aqua
Back Stitch

dark brown
Stem Stitch

brown
Stem Stitch

pink
Satin Stitch

white
Straight Stitch

turquoise
Back Stitch

aqua
Straight Stitch

aqua
French Knot

red
Back Stitch

aqua
French Knot

SNOWFLAKE SLIPPERS

Keep your tootsies cozy in these comfy embroidered slippers.

PROJECT DESIGNER: AIMEE RAY

WHAT YOU NEED

Embroidery Toolbox (page 9)

White terry-cloth slippers

Embroidery floss, 1 skein each of aqua and blue*

Heavy tissue or tracing paper

Motif: 088

Aimee used DMC embroidery floss colors 598 and 793.

STITCHES

Back Stitch

Straight Stitch

INSTRUCTIONS

1. Trace the snowflake motif from the CD or page 97 onto the tissue or tracing paper two times. Cut out the motifs, leaving a bit of extra paper around the edge of each.

2. Pin one of the tissue paper motifs to the outside top of each slipper.

3. Embroider the motifs using six threads of floss, through both the fabric and the paper at once. When you're done, carefully tear away the paper and use tweezers or your needle to remove any tiny bits that remain.

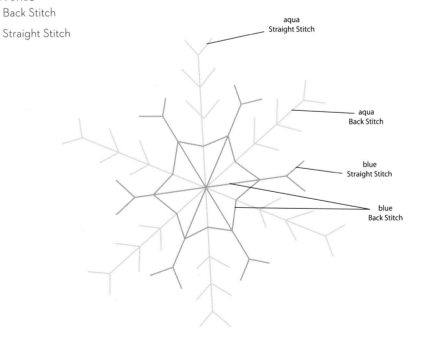

aqua
Straight Stitch

aqua
Back Stitch

blue
Straight Stitch

blue
Back Stitch

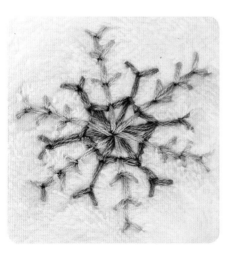

LET IT SNOW GARLAND

Here's a versatile garland you can drape anywhere for a bit of cheer. Or make several shorter garlands of different lengths and hang them vertically.

PROJECT DESIGNER: AIMEE RAY

WHAT YOU NEED

Embroidery Toolbox (page 9)

Templates (page 125)

Blue, aqua, and white felt scraps

Aqua patterned fabric scraps

Embroidery floss, 1 skein each of aqua and white*

Pinking shears

White fabric or craft glue

White satin ribbon, ¼ inch (6 mm) wide and 90 inches (2.28 m) long

Motifs: 095, 097

*Aimee used DMC embroidery floss in colors 3811 and white.

Finished Size: 90 inches (2.3 m)

STITCHES

French Knot

Straight Stitch

INSTRUCTIONS

1. Use the templates to cut circles from the felt and fabric with the pinking shears. Cut two pieces, a front and a back, for each snowflake circle on your garland, plus another small circle for the center of each large circle. Use any fabrics you like, but it's a good idea to use felt for the back of each circle to make the assemblage sturdy. For a 90-inch (2.28 m) garland, you'll need 20 large circles and 32 small circles total.

2. Embroider a snowflake or star in white or aqua onto each small circle front piece.

3. Use the fabric glue to attach a small circle to the front of each large circle. Use the fabric glue to attach the ribbon between the layers of each circle, spacing the circles 1 to 2 inches (2.5 to 5.1 cm) apart, and alternating large and small circles.

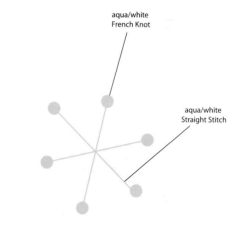

aqua/white
Straight Stitch

aqua/white
French Knot

aqua/white
Straight Stitch

FELT WINTER VILLAGE

Use the colors shown for this whimsical little felt village, and you can leave it up all year, or stitch it up in reds and greens for more of a Christmas scene.

PROJECT DESIGNER: AIMEE RAY

WHAT YOU NEED

Embroidery Toolbox (page 9)

Templates (page 129)

Felt in green, light green, dark green, brown, light brown, dark brown, and aqua (or colors of choice)

Embroidery floss, 1 skein each of aqua, light brown, brown, green, and dark green*

Polyester fiberfill stuffing

Motifs: 179, 180, 181, 182, 183, 184, 185, 186, 187, 188, 189, 190

*Aimee used DMC embroidery floss colors 598, 422, 434, 470, and 469.

Finished Size: 2½ to 3 inches (6.4 to 7.3 cm) tall

STITCHES

French Knot

Lazy Daisy

Satin Stitch

Scallop Stitch

Split Stitch

Straight Stitch

INSTRUCTIONS

1. Use the templates to cut all of the house and tree pieces from the felt. Use the photos for reference for the felt colors of each piece, or choose your own combinations.

2. Now decorate your house pieces. To attach the doors, pin the felt pieces in place and stitch them on using the Stab Stitch and two threads of floss that match the door color. Embroider the motifs from the CD or page 106 on each house piece according to the stitch guides, using three of the six threads of floss for each color. Since the motifs are so tiny, you might find it easiest to freehand them, but if you need a guide, the tissue paper method of transferring and stitching the motifs will work best. Feel free to mix and match the motifs to create your own unique houses.

3. Stitch the walls and front and back parts of each house together using the Whip Stitch and two threads of floss that match the house color. Whip Stitch the bottom piece on to make a box shape. Stitch on the roof pieces last, using two threads of floss that match the roof color. Leave a small space open.

4. Stuff the house with a small amount of the stuffing—don't add so much that the walls bulge out. Stitch up the hole.

5. For each tree, first transfer and embroider the motifs according to the stitch guide. Then fold the tree in half lengthwise and stitch up the back seam using the Whip Stitch. Stuff a bit of fiberfill inside. The trees will stand up nicely without a bottom piece.

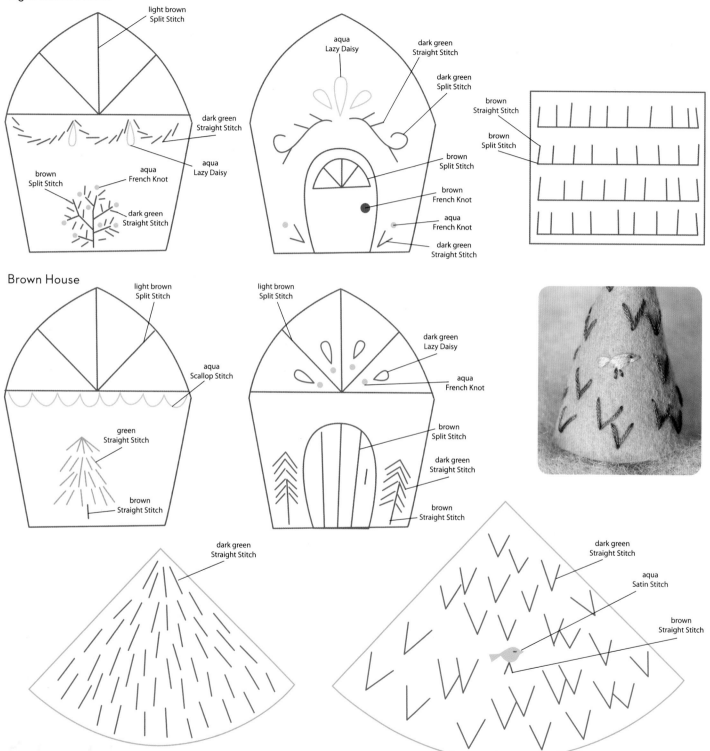

Light Green House

light brown
Split Stitch

dark green
Straight Stitch

aqua
Lazy Daisy

brown
Split Stitch

aqua
French Knot

dark green
Straight Stitch

aqua
Lazy Daisy

dark green
Straight Stitch

dark green
Split Stitch

brown
Split Stitch

brown
French Knot

aqua
French Knot

dark green
Straight Stitch

brown
Straight Stitch

brown
Split Stitch

Brown House

light brown
Split Stitch

aqua
Scallop Stitch

green
Straight Stitch

brown
Straight Stitch

light brown
Split Stitch

dark green
Lazy Daisy

aqua
French Knot

brown
Split Stitch

dark green
Straight Stitch

brown
Straight Stitch

dark green
Straight Stitch

dark green
Straight Stitch

aqua
Satin Stitch

brown
Straight Stitch

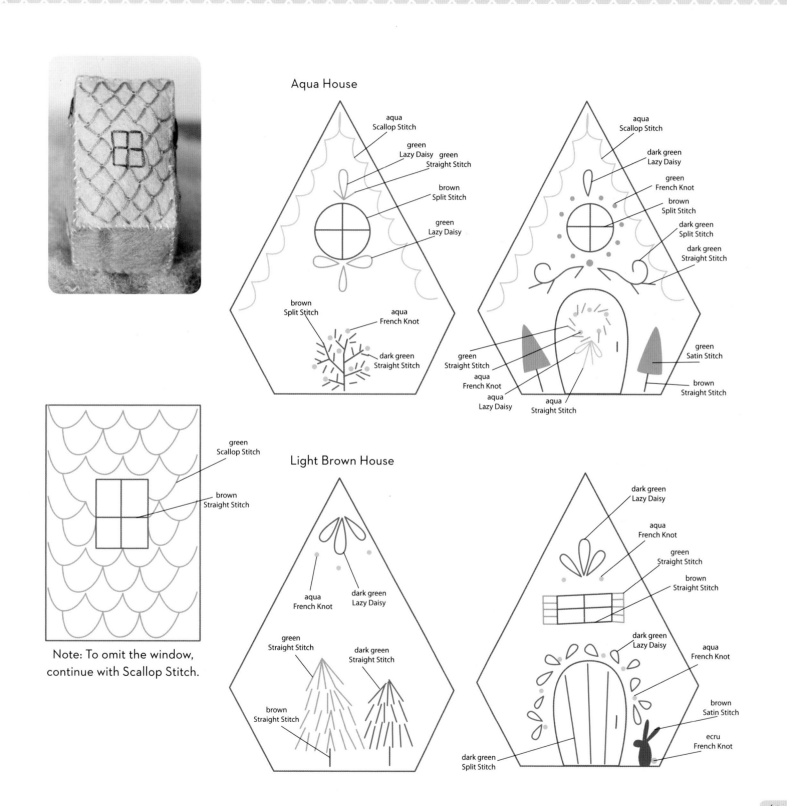

Aqua House

aqua
Scallop Stitch

green
Lazy Daisy   green
Straight Stitch

brown
Split Stitch

green
Lazy Daisy

brown
Split Stitch

aqua
French Knot

dark green
Straight Stitch

aqua
Scallop Stitch

dark green
Lazy Daisy

green
French Knot

brown
Split Stitch

dark green
Split Stitch

dark green
Straight Stitch

green
Straight Stitch

aqua
French Knot

aqua
Lazy Daisy

aqua
Straight Stitch

green
Satin Stitch

brown
Straight Stitch

green
Scallop Stitch

brown
Straight Stitch

Note: To omit the window,
continue with Scallop Stitch.

Light Brown House

aqua
French Knot

dark green
Lazy Daisy

green
Straight Stitch

dark green
Straight Stitch

brown
Straight Stitch

dark green
Lazy Daisy

aqua
French Knot

green
Straight Stitch

brown
Straight Stitch

dark green
Lazy Daisy

aqua
French Knot

brown
Satin Stitch

ecru
French Knot

dark green
Split Stitch

WINTER WOODS MINIATURE TREE SKIRT

This little hand-sewn tree skirt with a forest theme
is perfect for a small tabletop tree.

PROJECT DESIGNER: AIMEE RAY

WHAT YOU NEED

Embroidery Toolbox (page 9)

Templates (page 126)

White felt, 12 x 18 inches (30.5 x 45.7 cm)

Light green felt, 12 x 18 inches (30.5 x 45.7 cm)

Olive green felt, 9 x 12 inches (22.9 x 30.5 cm), or scraps

Tissue paper

Embroidery floss, 1 skein each of dark green, green, dark brown, brown, and white*

White sewing thread

Motifs: 091, 114, 115, 116, 117, 200, 201, 202, 203

*Aimee used DMC embroidery floss colors 469, 470, 433, 434, and white.

Finished Size: 11¾ inches (30 cm) diameter

STITCHES

Back Stitch

French Knot

Scallop Stitch

Stab Stitch

Straight Stitch

INSTRUCTIONS

1. Using the templates, trace and cut the two circular shapes, one each from the white and light green felt. Trace and cut four triangles for trees from the olive green felt.

2. Using the photos for reference, position the white piece over the green circle (it will be slightly larger) and use the Stab Stitch and the white sewing thread to attach it. Then position the four felt tree shapes in place and embroider them according to the stitch guide to attach them.

3. Trace the animal and tree motifs from the CD or pages 99 and 108 onto tissue paper and pin them in place on the tree skirt, using the photo for reference. Embroider the motifs according to the stitch guide. When you're finished, gently tear away the tissue paper. Use tweezers or your needle to remove any little stuck pieces of tissue paper.

4. Embellish the green felt by embroidering scattered snowflakes, using Straight Stitches and French Knots with the white floss.

NOEL WALL HANGING

Bedeck your front door or an eye-catching wall with this beautiful celebration of the season.

PROJECT DESIGNER: TERESA MAIRAL BARREU

WHAT YOU NEED

Embroidery Toolbox (page 9)

White quilter's cotton, 23 x 10 inches (58.4 x 25.4 cm)

Patterned fabric:

- Two 22¼ x 3½ inch (56.5 x 8.9 cm) pieces
- Two 14⅞ x 3½ inch (37.8 x 8.9 cm) pieces
- Two scraps to cover 19 mm self-covered buttons

Red fabric:

- One 90 x 2½-inch (228.6 x 6.4 cm) strips (for the binding)
- Two 9 x 4-inch (22.9 x 10.2 cm) strips (for the hanging tabs)

Muslin or scrap fabric for backing, 30 x 17 inches (76.2 x 43.2 cm)

Batting, 30 x 17 inches (76.2 x 43.2 cm)

Embroidery floss, 1 skein red*

Self-covered button kit for ¾-inch (19 mm) buttons (you'll need 2 buttons)

Motifs: 011, 204

*Teresa used DMC embroidery floss color 321a.

Finished Size: 27¼ x 14½ inches (69.2 x 36.8 cm)

STITCHES

Back Stitch

French Knot

Satin Stitch

Slip Stitch

Stem Stitch

Straight Stitch

INSTRUCTIONS

Note: Quilting Essentials can be found starting on page 23.

1. Transfer the motifs from the CD or pages 93 and 108 to the white quilter's cotton and embroider with three threads of the red floss according to the stitch guide.

2. After embroidering, cut the fabric to 22¼ x 8⅞ inches (56.5 x 22.5 cm) with the design centered.

3. Stitch one of the 22¼ x 3½-inch (56.5 x 8.9 cm) strips of patterned fabric to each side of the embroidered rectangle. Then stitch one of the 14⅞ x 3½-inch (37.8 x 8.9 cm) strips of patterned fabric to the top and one to the bottom of the assemblage.

4. Make a "quilt sandwich" (page 23) by layering the 30 x 17 inch (76.2 x 43.2 cm) backing piece (right side down), the 30 x 17-inch (76.2 x 43.2 cm) piece of batting, and the patchwork (right side up) together to prepare for quilting. Baste or pin, and then quilt as desired. (The project shown was quilted with free-motion stipling [page 24]).

5. After quilting, trim the batting ⅛ inch (3 mm) from the edge of the quilt top.

6. Now it's time to attach the binding (see page 25 for a refresher on making and attaching binding). First, fold the binding strip in half lengthwise, wrong sides together. Iron it flat. Once the whole strip is ironed, align the raw edges with the edge of the quilt top, pin, and stitch ¼ inch (6 mm) from the edge all around the piece with mitered corners. Fold the binding to the back of the piece and pin it in place. Slip Stitch the binding to the back of the piece, mitering the corners as you go.

7. Follow the manufacturer's instructions in your self-covered button kit to cover two buttons with the patterned fabric.

8. To make the hanging tabs, first fold each 9 x 4-inch (22.9 x 10.2 cm) strip lengthwise with right sides facing in. Stitch around two sides, leaving one short side open. Trim the corners, turn the tube right side out, and press flat. Turn the open edge inside and stitch it closed. Fold each tab in half and position on the front and back of the hanging, using the photo for reference (they're about 3½ inches [8.9 cm] in from the sides and 1½ inches [3.8 cm] down from the top of the hanging). Center a button on each tab and attach both the tabs and the buttons to the piece by stitching through the front tabs, the quilted hanging, and the back tabs.

Stem Stitch

French Knot

Back/Satin
Stitch

Straight Stitch

Straight Stitch

Stem Stitch

Straight Stitch

French Knot

Straight Stitch

Stem Stitch

PLUSH VINTAGE ORNAMENTS

Sweet plush ornaments make perfect gifts, and these vintage-inspired characters add cheer to any holiday style.

PROJECT DESIGNER: AIMEE RAY

WHAT YOU NEED

(for each ornament)

Embroidery Toolbox (page 9)

Templates (page 125)

White quilter's cotton fabric, 6 inches (15.2 cm) square

Red or green fabric, 6 inches (15.2 cm) square (for backing)

Embroidery floss, 1 skein each of red, pink, light green, green, light brown, dark brown, and peach*

Red or green ribbon, ¼ inch (6 mm) wide and 6 inches (15.2 cm) in length

White sewing thread

Polyester fiberfill stuffing

Motifs: 113, 156, 212

*Aimee used DMC embroidery floss in colors 321, 760, 906, 907, 435, 3787, and 950.

Finished Size: 2¾ to 4½ inches (7 to 11.4 cm) tall

STITCHES

Satin Stitch

Scallop Stitch

Split Stitch

Straight Stitch

INSTRUCTIONS

1. Transfer the motif from the CD or pages 99, 103, or 109 to the center of the white square of fabric and embroider according to the pattern.

2. Pin the embroidered white fabric to a colored piece, right sides facing. Trace the template onto the back of the white fabric, around your embroidery.

3. Loop the ribbon and pin it in place so its ends overlap the top of the template line. Then sew on the template line, leaving a 2-inch (5.1 cm) opening for turning at the bottom.

4. Turn the ornament right side out and stuff it firmly with the fiberfill stuffing. Stitch up the opening using the Hidden Stitch (page 21).

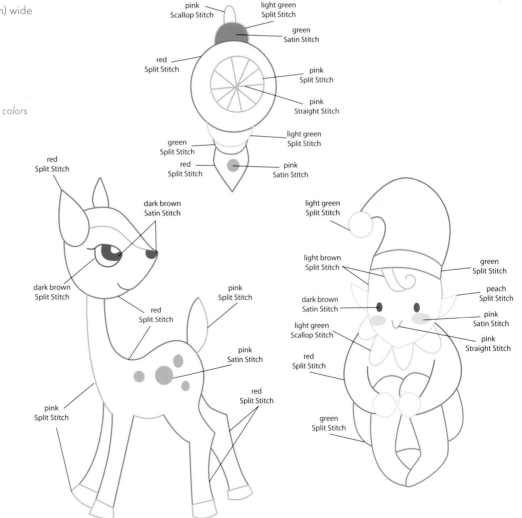

pink
Scallop Stitch

light green
Split Stitch

green
Satin Stitch

red
Split Stitch

pink
Split Stitch

pink
Straight Stitch

green
Split Stitch

light green
Split Stitch

red
Split Stitch

pink
Satin Stitch

red
Split Stitch

dark brown
Satin Stitch

dark brown
Split Stitch

red
Split Stitch

pink
Split Stitch

pink
Satin Stitch

red
Split Stitch

pink
Split Stitch

light green
Split Stitch

light brown
Split Stitch

green
Split Stitch

dark brown
Satin Stitch

peach
Split Stitch

light green
Scallop Stitch

pink
Satin Stitch

pink
Straight Stitch

red
Split Stitch

green
Split Stitch

PEACE ON EARTH CARD & GIFT TAG

Embroidering on paper is a fun way to add crisp, clean edges to your work. Give the gift tag with a present, and then use it to pretty up your tree as an ornament.

PROJECT DESIGNER: AIMEE RAY

WHAT YOU NEED

Embroidery Toolbox (page 9)

Template (page 125)

Cold press, heavyweight (140 lb.) watercolor paper or heavy card stock

Embroidery floss, 1 skein each of green, light green, aqua, light aqua, and dark blue*

Motifs: 001, 110

Aimee used DMC embroidery floss colors 471, 472, 598, 3811, and 924.

Finished Size:
Card Front: 5 x 4 inches (12.7 x 10.2 cm)
Gift Tag: 2¼ inches (5.7 cm) diameter

STITCHES

Back Stitch

Satin Stitch

Whip Stitch

INSTRUCTIONS

1. Cut a 5 x 8-inch (12.7 x 20.3 cm) piece of watercolor paper. Lightly score it and fold it in half horizontally. Use the circle surrounding the dove design to cut a circle from the watercolor paper.

2. Trace the motifs from the CD or pages 92 and 99 onto the paper using a light table or a sunny window.

3. Separate your floss, and use three of the six threads to stitch every part of the motifs except for the outline of the earth—use all six threads there. The Back Stitch is ideal for embroidering on paper. Just keep your stitches a little longer than usual so that the paper doesn't tear in between stitches. If you have trouble getting the needle to come up in the right place from the underside of the paper, poke holes through from the top side of the paper first.

4. Stitch around the edge of the card front and the gift tag using the Whip Stitch (page 22).

5. Stitch a loop with two or three threads of the light green floss at the top of the gift tag.

dark blue Back Stitch

green Back Stitch

light aqua Back Stitch

dark blue Back Stitch

aqua Back Stitch

light green Back Stitch

green Satin Stitch

green Back Stitch

dark blue Back Stitch

peace on earth

FABRIC GIFT WRAP

Reusable fabric gift wrap, gift bags, and gift card sleeves are easy eco-friendly wrapping options. Make multiples in an array of colorful patterns for gift-giving all year long!

PROJECT DESIGNER: AIMEE RAY

WHAT YOU NEED

Embroidery Toolbox (page 9)

A variety of fabrics:

- 2 pieces, 10 x 10 inches (25.4 x 25.4 cm) (for the gift bag, see Note)
- 1 piece, 9½ x 5 inches (24.1 x 12.7 cm) (for the gift card Sleeve)
- 1 piece, size will vary depending on package to be wrapped (for the gift wrap)

Embroidery floss, 1 skein each of light green, green, dark green, red, dark pink, and white*

Satin or grosgrain ribbon, 1 inch (2.5 cm) wide and 36 inches (.91 m) long (for the gift bag)

Satin or grosgrain ribbon, ¼ inch (6 mm) wide and 24 inches (61 cm) long (for the gift card sleeve)

Large safety pin

Large beads or buttons

Motifs: 167, 168, 169, 170, 171

Note: These instructions are for a 7 x 8-inch (17.8 x 20.3 cm) gift bag, but you can adjust the size to create any size bag you need.

Aimee used DMC embroidery floss in colors 907, 906, 905, 321, 3712, and white.

Finished Size:
Gift Bag: 9½ x 8 inches (24.1 x 20.3 cm)
Gift Card Sleeve: 3½ x 4 inches (8.9 x 10.2 cm)

STITCHES

Back Stitch

French Knot

Stem Stitch

Satin Stitch

INSTRUCTIONS

To Make the Gift Bag

1. Transfer and stitch an embroidery motif from the CD or page 104 to the bottom center or the bottom corner of one of the two 10-inch (25.4 cm) squares of fabric.

2. Position the embroidered square of fabric right side up, with the embellishment at the bottom. Place the plain square of fabric on top of this piece so the pieces are now right sides together. Sew down one side.

3. Open the resulting long piece of fabric and place it right side down. Fold down 1 inch (2.5 cm) of the top long edge to the wrong side to create the channel for the ribbon, and hem it.

4. Fold the piece back in half with right sides facing, and sew around the bottom and remaining side, stopping short of the hem opening at the top. Trim the corners and flip the bag right side out.

5. Pin the safety pin onto one end of the 1-inch (2.5 cm) wide ribbon and thread it through the channel at the top of the bag.

6. To prevent the ribbon from sliding back inside the hem when the gift bag is opened, tie a large bead or sew a large button onto each end of the ribbon if desired.

x x x x x x x x x x x x x x x x x x x x x x

TIP

Dark fabric hides what's inside best, but if you want to use a light color, cut two pieces of white fabric to use as a liner, match them up with each colored square, and then sew as though each set were one piece of fabric.

x x x x x x x x x x x x x x x x x x x x x x

hem →

wrong side

hem →

figure 1

To Make the Gift Card Sleeve

1. Transfer and stitch an embroidery motif from the CD or page 104 onto the front of the 9½ x 5-inch (24.1 x 12.7 cm) piece of fabric, positioned as desired.

2. Place the fabric right side down and hem each short end of the piece ½ inch (1.3 cm) (figure 1).

3. Fold the short ends right sides in, so that they overlap each other as shown in figure 2, and create a 4-inch (10.2 cm) rectangle.

4. Sew up the sides, trim the corners, and flip the sleeve right side out (figure 3). To slide a gift card inside, flip the top end inside out, slide the card inside, then flip it back over. If you want to embellish the card sleeve, tie on the ¼-inch (6 mm) wide ribbon.

For the Gift Wrap

1. Measure and cut a piece of fabric to the size needed to wrap a gift just as you would with paper gift wrap. Wrap the gift and determine where you'd like the embroidered motif to go.

2. Unwrap the fabric, and transfer and stitch the motif from the CD or page 104. Rewrap the gift and secure with tape, just as you would with paper gift wrap.

sew →

wrong side

← sew

figure 2

figure 3

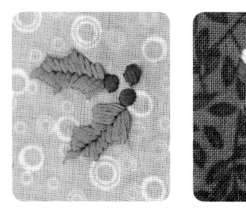

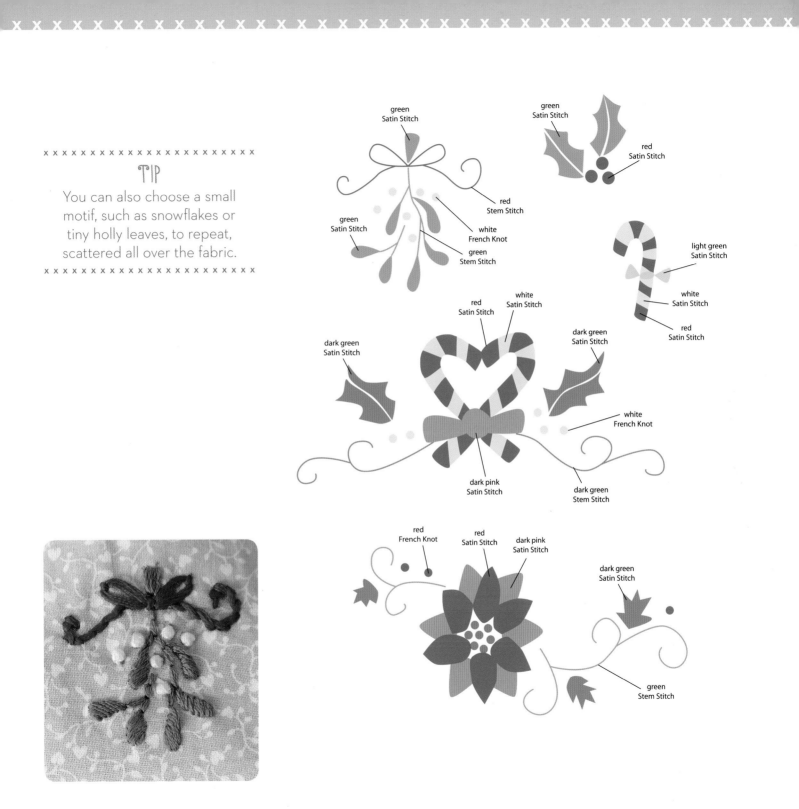

TIP

You can also choose a small motif, such as snowflakes or tiny holly leaves, to repeat, scattered all over the fabric.

green Satin Stitch

green Satin Stitch

red Stem Stitch

white French Knot

green Satin Stitch

green Stem Stitch

green Satin Stitch

red Satin Stitch

light green Satin Stitch

white Satin Stitch

red Satin Stitch

red Satin Stitch

white Satin Stitch

dark green Satin Stitch

dark green Satin Stitch

white French Knot

dark pink Satin Stitch

dark green Stem Stitch

red French Knot

red Satin Stitch

dark pink Satin Stitch

dark green Satin Stitch

green Stem Stitch

TEASHOP TEAPOT COZY

Pair your favorite hot tea with the cheery sights and scents of a sweet shop! Each side of this adorable embroidered and appliquéd teapot cozy is embellished with charming detail, and your teapot's spout and handle each have their own little door.

PROJECT DESIGNER: ANNIE KIGHT

WHAT YOU NEED

Embroidery Toolbox (page 9)

Templates (page 130)

White wool-blend felt, two 12 x 18-inch (30.5 x 45.7 cm) sheets

Light pink wool-blend felt, two 12 x 18-inch (30.5 x 45.7 cm) sheets

Aqua wool-blend felt, one 12 x 18-inch (30.5 x 45.7 cm) sheet

Lime green wool-blend felt, one 12 x 18-inch (30.5 x 45.7 cm) sheet

Tissue paper

Embroidery floss, 1 skein each of turquoise, red, light pink, aqua, pink, light green, green, brown, and white*

White sewing thread

3 buttons (1 for the doorknob, 1 for each roof peak)

Motifs: 067, 208, 209, 248, 249, 250, 251, 252, 253, 254

*Annie used DMC embroidery floss colors 597, 321, 3713, 598, 760, 907, 905, 433, and white.

Finished Size: 5½ x 5½ x 6½ inches (14 x 14 x 16.5 cm)

STITCHES

Back Stitch

Blanket Stitch

French Knot

Satin Stitch

Straight Stitch

Whip Stitch

ADJUSTING FOR YOUR TEAPOT SIZE

This cozy was sized for a 5½ x 5½ x 6½-inch (14 x 14 x 16.5 cm) teapot with the lid in place. If your teapot is a lot bigger or smaller (or has a different shaped spout or handle), you'll need to adjust the templates. (If your teapot is quite a bit bigger, you might also need more felt.) Adapt the shop's door and back opening, and enlarge or decrease the size of the wall and roof templates by taking the following measurements:

- Measure from the base of your teapot to its rim to determine the height of the teashop's walls.
- Measure the length and width of your teapot's globe to determine the length and width of the teashop's walls.
- Measure from the teapot's rim to the top of its lid to determine the pitch of the teashop's roof.
- Measure the height and width of your teapot's spout to determine the height and width of the teashop's door.
- Measure the height and width of your teapot's handle to determine the height and width of the teashop's back opening.

INSTRUCTIONS

Constructing the Walls and the Door

1. Using the wall templates (A through D), cut one piece for each wall from the white felt and one matching piece for each wall from the pink felt.

2. Pin each set of pink and white A through D pieces together with the pink felt on the bottom and the white felt on the top. Machine-stitch around the outer edge of each piece with a 1/4-inch (6 mm) seam allowance, but leave the bottoms open. Trim the corners and turn each piece inside out.

3. Arrange the pieces as shown in figure 1, making sure that the white sides are facing up and the open end of each piece is at the bottom. If you are using wool-blend felt, press the pieces flat with an iron set on wool and a little steam. (If you are using acrylic felt, press the pieces carefully with the iron on a low setting; otherwise the felt can melt!)

4. Using figure 1 for reference again, Blanket Stitch the right side of piece C to the left side of piece A with two threads of red floss. Try to stitch only through the pink layer of felt and not the white; this will allow a little of the pink felt to peek through at the edges of the house once it's upright and the white sides are facing out as in the photos. Then Blanket Stitch the right side of piece A to the left side of piece D, and finally the right side of D to the left side of B, again using two threads of red floss and stitching through the pink layer of felt only.

5. You might be tempted at this point to stitch the right side of B to the left side of C, but don't! Instead, lay the panels flat, white sides up. Felt has a tendency to stretch, so now is a good time to carefully trim the bottom edges so that all the pieces line up. Be careful, however, not to overtrim or your teashop will be too short when completed.

6. Use the door template to cut two matching doors from the aqua felt. Back Stitch with two threads of the light pink floss to add the look of wood panels onto the front of one door piece. Then sew a cute button on this same piece to mimic a doorknob. Place this embellished door piece right side up onto the plain door piece and Blanket Stitch around the edges using two threads of aqua floss. Whip Stitch the left edge of the door to the left side of the opening in wall piece C using a single thread of aqua floss.

Making the Embroidered Appliqué Patches

1. As you can see from the photos, each appliqué patch consists of a white felt shape, which is embroidered and then Whip Stitched to a matching, but larger, colored felt shape. Begin by using the templates to cut all of the white and colored felt shapes. Place each white shape by its slightly larger colored shape to stay organized.

2. Trace the following motifs from the CD or pages 95, 108, and 113 onto tissue paper: one teapot, two holiday trees, one teashop window, one teacup, two topiaries, and one sitting window. Be sure to leave enough room in between them so you can cut each out with a border for pinning onto the felt.

3. Cut the traced motifs out roughly, pin each onto the center of its white shape, and embroider according to the stitch guides. Gently tear away the tissue paper and remove any little stuck pieces with tweezers or your needle. Whip Stitch each embroidered white patch onto its corresponding slightly larger colored patch using one thread of white floss.

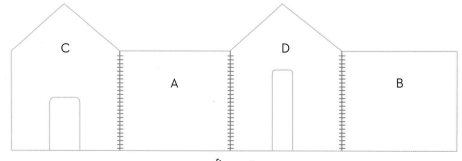

figure 1

Attaching the Appliqué Patches

1. For wall C: Pin the teapot appliqué patch above the doorway and Whip Stitch it in place using one thread of light pink floss. Then pin each holiday tree appliqué onto either side of the doorway, about ¼ inch (6 mm) up from the bottom, and Whip Stitch it in place with one thread of light green floss.

2 For wall A: Pin the teashop window appliqué onto piece A and Whip Stitch it into place using one thread of aqua floss. Using the template, cut awning A from the pink felt, and Blanket Stitch around its scalloped edge with two threads of red floss. Pin the pink awning above the teashop window and Whip Stitch it in place with one thread of light pink floss. To create a three-dimensional effect, fold the edges of the awning around the top edges of the window while stitching it in place.

3. For wall D (shown on page 88): Pin the teacup appliqué above the opening (where the teapot handle will poke out) and Whip Stitch it in place with one thread of light pink floss. Then Whip Stitch each topiary appliqué on either side of the opening, about ¼ inch (6 mm) from the bottom, with one thread of light green floss.

4. For wall B (shown on page 84): Pin the table and chairs appliqué patch into place about ¼ inch (6 mm) from the bottom. Whip Stitch it into place using one thread of aqua floss. Using the template, cut awning B from the pink felt, and Blanket Stitch around

its scalloped edge with two threads of red floss, just as you did for awning A. Whip Stitch it above the table and chairs patch using one thread of light pink floss. To create a three-dimensional effect, fold the edges of the awning around the top edges of the appliqué patch while stitching in place.

5. Now you can finally Blanket Stitch the right side of wall B to the left side of wall C, using two threads of red floss and stitching only through the pink layer of felt.

Making the Roof

1. Use the template to cut four roof pieces from the pink felt. Trace the roof template, including the polka dots, onto tissue paper two times, cut the traced templates out, and pin each one onto one pink roof piece. Embroider each polka dot by using six threads of the aqua floss to make a French Knot. When done, gently tear away the tissue paper.

2. Align each embroidered roof piece right side down onto a plain roof piece, pin, and sew along the outside edges with a ¼ inch (6 mm) seam allowance, but leave the scalloped sides open. Turn each roof piece inside out and press with the iron.

3. Align the two roof pieces, right sides out, and Blanket Stitch them together on their long unscalloped edges using two threads of the red floss. Then Blanket Stitch the scalloped edges of each roof piece using two threads of the red floss.

4. Place the roof onto the top of the teashop, making sure to line up the pitch of the roof with the very top point of walls C and D. Secure it in place with a few basting stitches or pins. Using two threads of red floss, Blanket Stitch the roof onto the top of wall C, making sure you begin and end about 1 inch (2.5 cm) from the scalloped edge so that the ends of the roof hang free over the sides of the house. Now repeat this to attach the roof to the top of wall D.

5. Sew a decorative button to each roof peak.

Finishing the Teashop Cozy

As a final step, Blanket Stitch all the way around the bottom of the teashop using one thread of white floss. Tack all four corners on the inside to help the cozy stand upright. Now put on the kettle, and make a pot of tea to keep cozy!

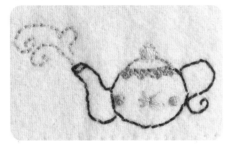

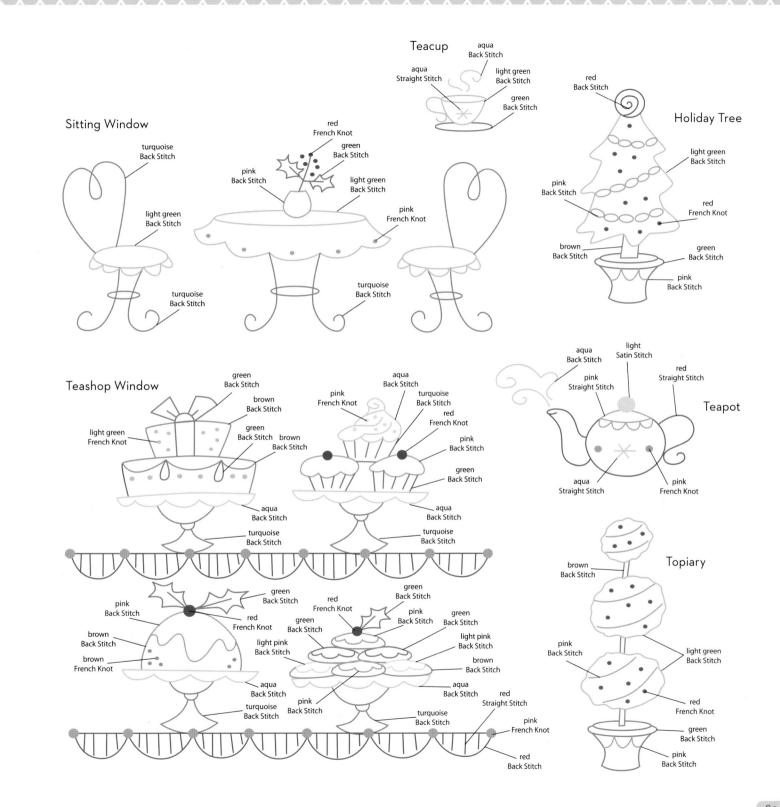

Sitting Window

turquoise Back Stitch

light green Back Stitch

turquoise Back Stitch

pink Back Stitch

red French Knot

green Back Stitch

light green Back Stitch

pink French Knot

turquoise Back Stitch

Teacup

aqua Straight Stitch

aqua Back Stitch

light green Back Stitch

green Back Stitch

Holiday Tree

red Back Stitch

light green Back Stitch

pink Back Stitch

red French Knot

brown Back Stitch

green Back Stitch

pink Back Stitch

Teashop Window

green Back Stitch

brown Back Stitch

green Back Stitch

light green French Knot

brown Back Stitch

pink French Knot

aqua Back Stitch

turquoise Back Stitch

red French Knot

pink Back Stitch

green Back Stitch

aqua Back Stitch

turquoise Back Stitch

pink Back Stitch

green Back Stitch

red French Knot

brown Back Stitch

brown French Knot

light pink Back Stitch

aqua Back Stitch

turquoise Back Stitch

green Back Stitch

green Back Stitch

red French Knot

pink Back Stitch

green Back Stitch

light pink Back Stitch

brown Back Stitch

aqua Back Stitch

pink Back Stitch

turquoise Back Stitch

red Straight Stitch

pink French Knot

red Back Stitch

aqua Back Stitch

light Satin Stitch

red Straight Stitch

pink Straight Stitch

Teapot

aqua Straight Stitch

pink French Knot

Topiary

brown Back Stitch

pink Back Stitch

light green Back Stitch

red French Knot

green Back Stitch

pink Back Stitch

GINGERBREAD BOOKMARKS

These gingerbread cookie bookmarks would also make great ornaments—just add
a loop of narrow ribbon to the backing felt instead of the gingham ribbon.

PROJECT DESIGNER: LAURA HOWARD

WHAT YOU NEED

Embroidery Toolbox (page 9)

Brown felt, 9 x 12 inches (22.9 x 30.5 cm)

Tissue paper

Embroidery floss, 1 skein each of pink, black, and white*

Red gingham ribbon, ⅝ inch (1.6 m) wide and 22 inches (56 cm) long (see Note)

Brown sewing thread

Motifs: 245, 246

Laura used DMC embroidery floss colors 3713, 310, and white.

Note: This length of gingham works well with paperbacks, but you may want to cut a longer ribbon for a bookmark for larger books.

Finished Size: Figures are 2½ inches (6.4 cm) tall

STITCHES

Back Stitch

Satin Stitch

Whip Stitch

INSTRUCTIONS

1. Trace the motifs from the CD or page 112 onto the tissue paper, making sure you leave plenty of space between them.

2. Hoop the felt and pin the traced gingerbread motifs in the center. Embroider the gingerbread motifs according to the stitch guides, but wait to embroider the eyes, buttons, and cheeks—remember that you'll be cutting out each design separately, so take care not to carry your threads outside the outer lines of each design.

3. Carefully tear away the tissue paper. Use tweezers or your needle to remove any small or fiddly pieces.

4. Embroider the eyes, buttons, and cheeks according to the stitch guides.

5. Remove the felt from the hoop, and cut out both motifs, leaving a small "frame" of felt around the outside of each. Then use these newly cut-out shapes as templates to cut matching backing shapes from the felt.

6. Cut an 11-inch (28 cm) length of the gingham ribbon for each bookmark, and then cut one end of each length of ribbon into two points to help prevent fraying.

7. Place the straight end of one ribbon at the bottom of one backing felt piece so the ribbon overlaps the felt by about 1 inch (2.5 cm). Sew the end of the ribbon in position with brown sewing thread and the Whip Stitch, sewing into the felt but not through it. Repeat for the other ribbon and backing piece.

8. Pin the front and back of one gingerbread person together, so that the ribbon end you just stitched is sandwiched in between. Sew the edges of the shape together with the brown sewing thread using the Whip Stitch. Finish your stitching neatly at the back. Repeat with the other gingerbread person.

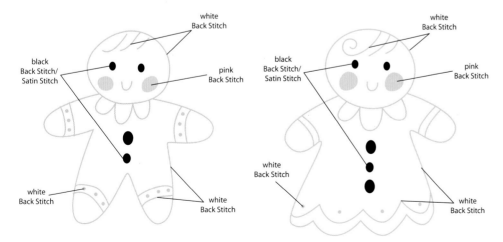

A YEAR OF HOLIDAY MOTIFS

TYPE

001
(Enlarge 200% for project)

002

003

004

005

not a creature was stirring...

006
(Enlarge 200% for project)

Peace ☆ Joy ☆ Love

007
(Enlarge 200% for project)

Christmas

008
(Enlarge 200% for project)

Jingle all the Way

009

'Tis the Season

010

011
(Enlarge 125% for project)

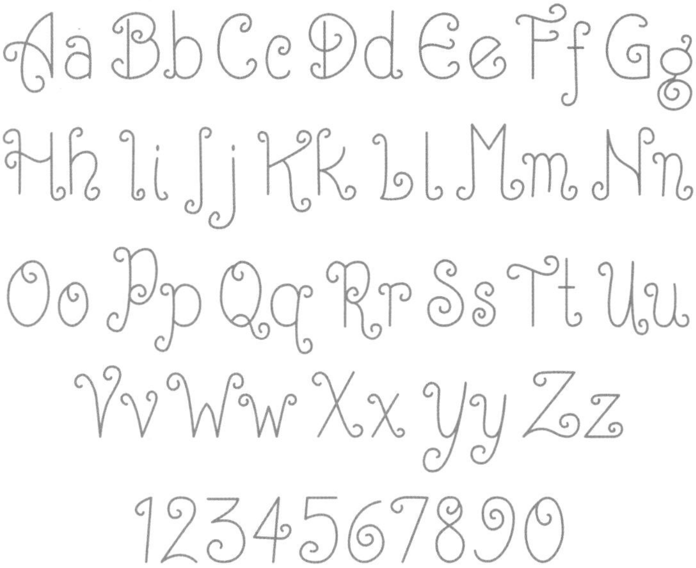

Aa Bb Cc Dd Ee Ff Gg
Hh Ii Jj Kk Ll Mm Nn
Oo Pp Qq Rr Ss Tt Uu
Vv Ww Xx Yy Zz
1234567890

012-038

Aa Bb Cc Dd Ee Ff Gg
Hh Ii Jj Kk Ll Mm Nn
Oo Pp Qq Rr Ss Tt Uu
Vv Ww Xx Yy Zz
1234567890

039-065

1 2 3 4 5
6 7 8 9 10
11 12 13 14 15
16 17 18 19 20
21 22 23 24 25

066
(Enlarge 125% for project)
Note: If you're making the Peace • Joy • Love
Advent Calendar on page 28, you'll need
to space these numbers evenly across your
strips of tissue paper.

94

BORDERS

067
(Actual size for project)

068

069

070

071

072

073
(Enlarge 200% for project)

074

075

076

077

078

079

080

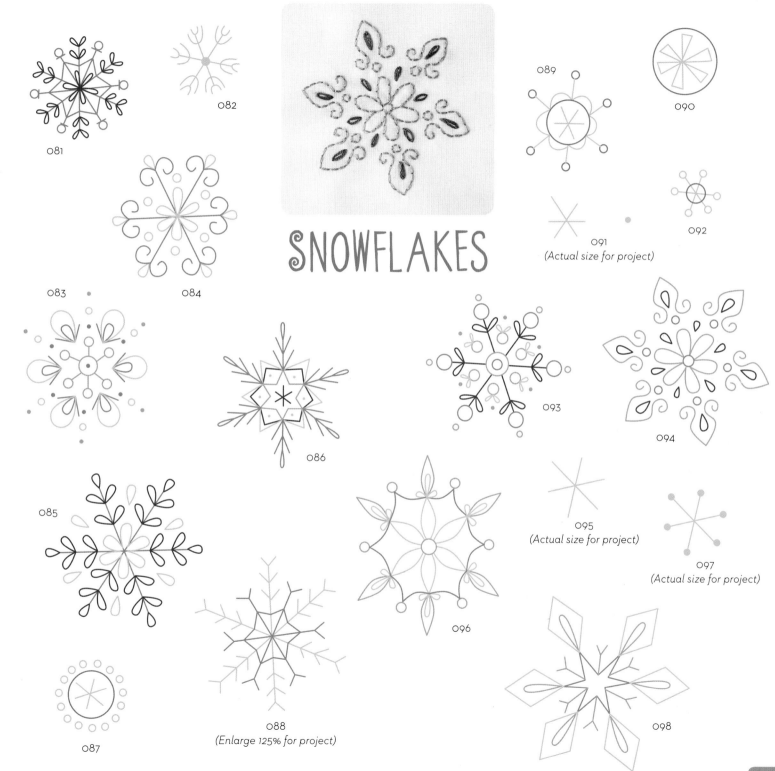

081

082

SNOWFLAKES

083

084

085

086

087

088
(Enlarge 125% for project)

089

090

091
(Actual size for project)

092

093

094

095
(Actual size for project)

096

097
(Actual size for project)

098

WINTER STARS

099

100

101

102

103

104

105
(Actual size for project)

106

107

108

109
(Actual size for project)

110
(Actual size for project)

111

112

113
(Actual size for project)

ANIMALS

114
(Actual size for project)

115
(Actual size for project)

116
(Actual size for project)

117
(Actual size for project)

118

119

120

121
(Actual size for project)

122

124

125

123

126

127
(Actual size for project)

128

129
(Enlarge 200% for project)

130
(Enlarge 200% for project)

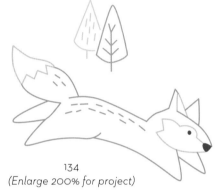

131
(Enlarge 200% for project)

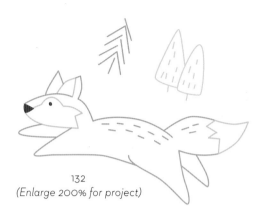

132
(Enlarge 200% for project)

133
(Enlarge 200% for project)

134
(Enlarge 200% for project)

135
(Enlarge 200% for project)

136

137

138

139

141

143

145

140

142

144

148
(Actual size for project)

146
(Actual size for project)

147
(Actual size for project)

149
(Actual size for project)

150
(Actual size for project)

151
(Actual size for project)

152

CHRISTMAS DECORATIONS

156
(Actual size for project)

153

154

155

159

157

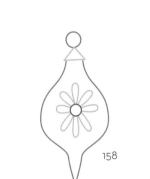

158

160

161

162

163

164

165

166

167
(Actual size for project)

168
(Actual size for project)

169
(Actual size for project)

170
(Actual size for project)

171
(Actual size for project)

172

173

174
(Enlarge 125% for project)

175

176
(Enlarge 125% for project)

177

178

(Enlarge all on this page 125% for project)

179

180

181

182

183

184

185

186

187

188

189

190

NUTCRACKER

191
192
193
194
195
196
197
198
199

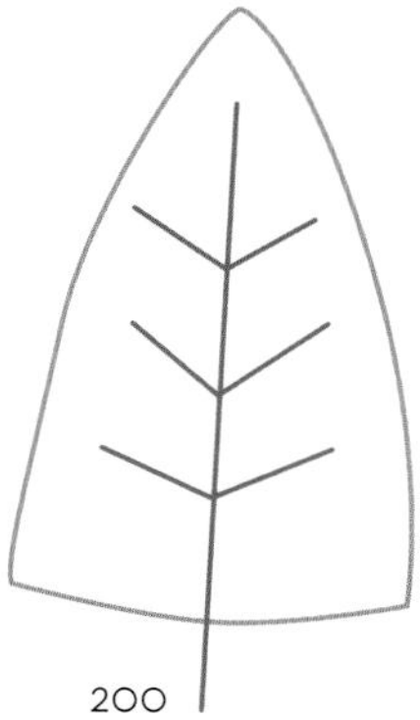

200
(Actual size for project)

201
(Actual size for project)

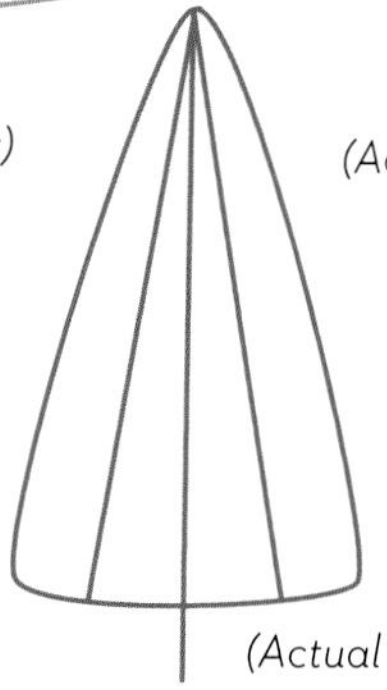

203
(Actual size for project)

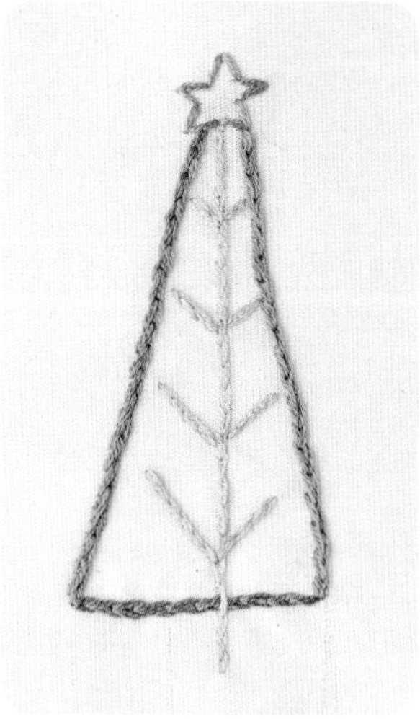

204
(Actual size for project)

202
(Actual size for project)

TREES

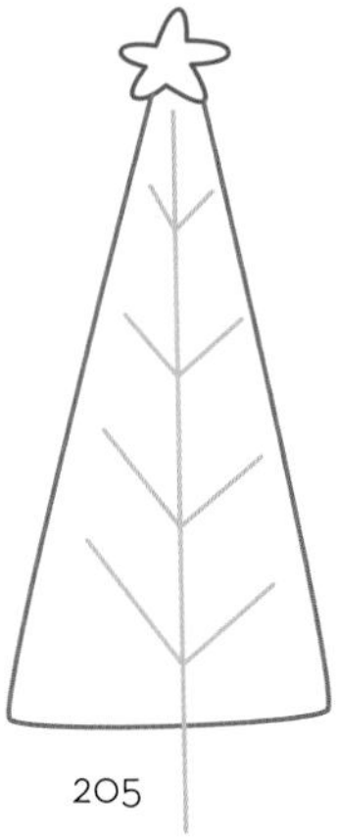

205

206

207

208
(Actual size for project)

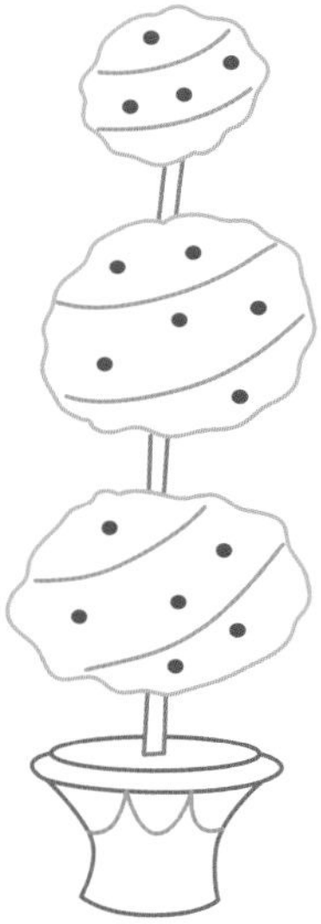

209
(Actual size for project)

210

211

CHRISTMAS CHARACTERS

212
(Actual size for project)

213

214

(Enlarge all on this page
125% for project)

216

217

215

218

219

220

221

222

223

224

225

226

227

228
(Actual size for project)

229
(Actual size for project)

230
(Actual size for project)

231
(Actual size for project)

232

234

235

236

237

233

238

CANDYLAND

244

239

243

240

241

242

245
(Actual size for project)

246
(Actual size for project)

247

249
(Actual size for project)

248
(Actual size for project)

250
(Actual size for project)

251
(Actual size for project)

252
(Actual size for project)

253
(Actual size for project)

254
(Actual size for project)

255

256

257

NEW YEAR

258

259

260

261

262

263

265

VALENTINE'S DAY

264

266

267

BE MINE

I'M YOURS

NO WAY

268

Love

270

271

272

269

ST. PATRICK'S DAY

273

274

275

276

277

278

279

280

281

283

282

EASTER & SPRING

EARTH DAY

mom

284

285

286

287

288

289

290

291

LOVE THE EARTH

292

293

294

295

296

297

298

4TH OF JULY & SUMMER

299

300

301

302

303

304

305

306

307

308

309

310

HALLOWEEN

311

312

313

314

315

316

317

318

319

320

DIA DE LOS MUERTOS

321

322

323

324

325

THANKSGIVING

326
(Actual size for project)

327

328

329

HANUKKAH

330

331

332

333

TEMPLATES

All of the project templates on the following pages can also be found at actual size on the CD. For PDF templates that span two pages or more, simply print the pages you need on 8½ x 11 inch (21.5 x 28 cm) paper, cut along the dotted lines, and align the edges by matching the letters together (A with A, B with B, and so on). Tape the pieces together, then cut them out.

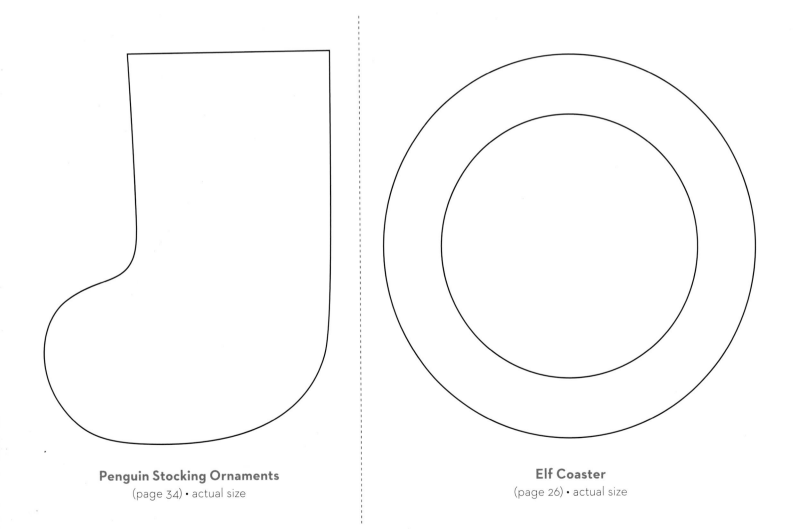

Penguin Stocking Ornaments
(page 34) • actual size

Elf Coaster
(page 26) • actual size

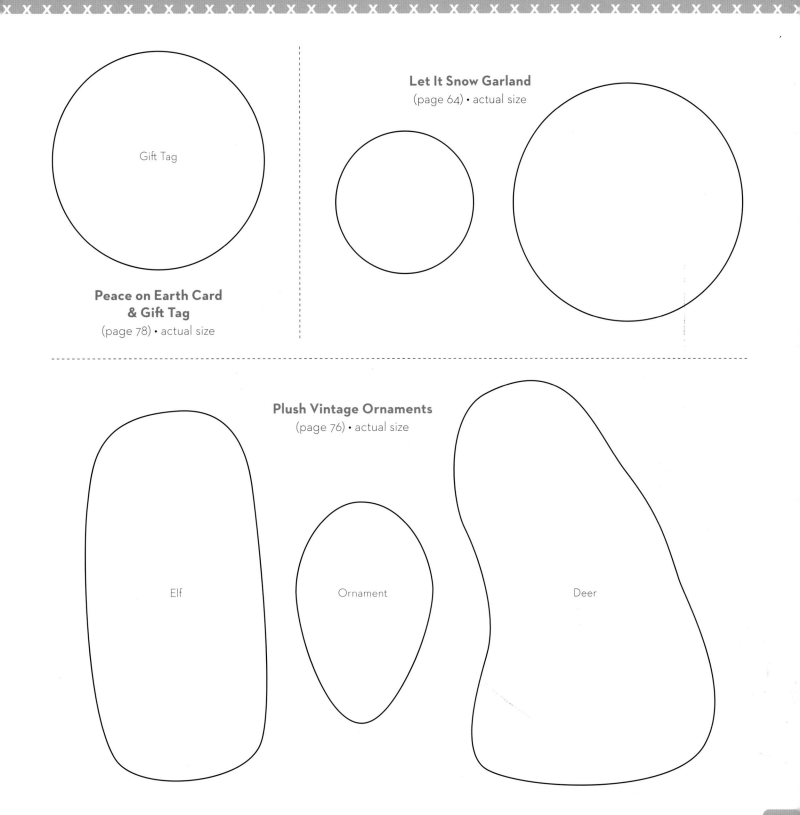

Gift Tag

Let It Snow Garland
(page 64) • actual size

**Peace on Earth Card
& Gift Tag**
(page 78) • actual size

Plush Vintage Ornaments
(page 76) • actual size

Elf

Ornament

Deer

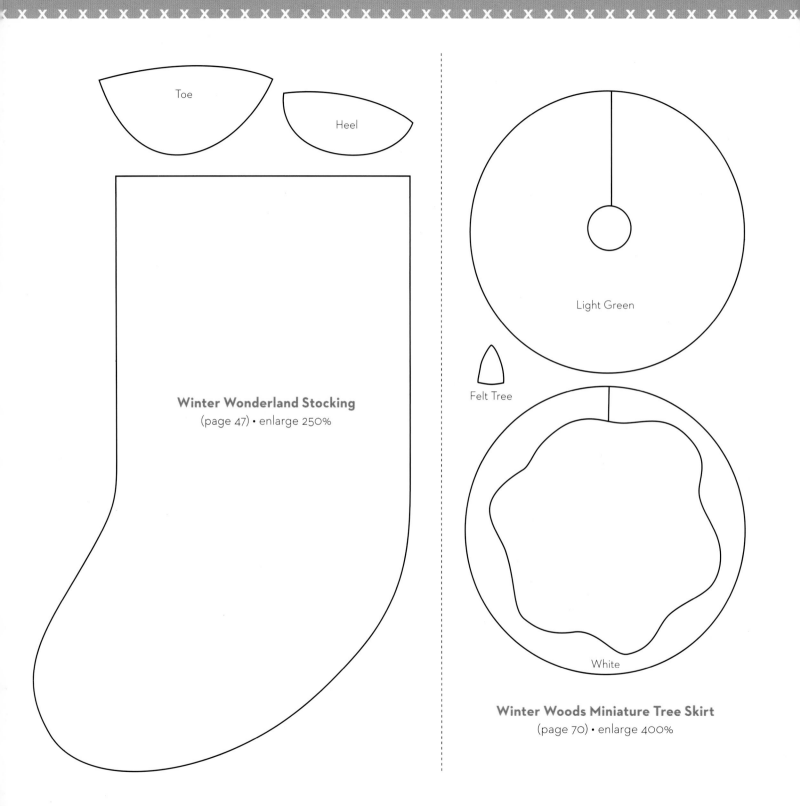

Toe

Heel

Winter Wonderland Stocking
(page 47) • enlarge 250%

Light Green

Felt Tree

White

Winter Woods Miniature Tree Skirt
(page 70) • enlarge 400%

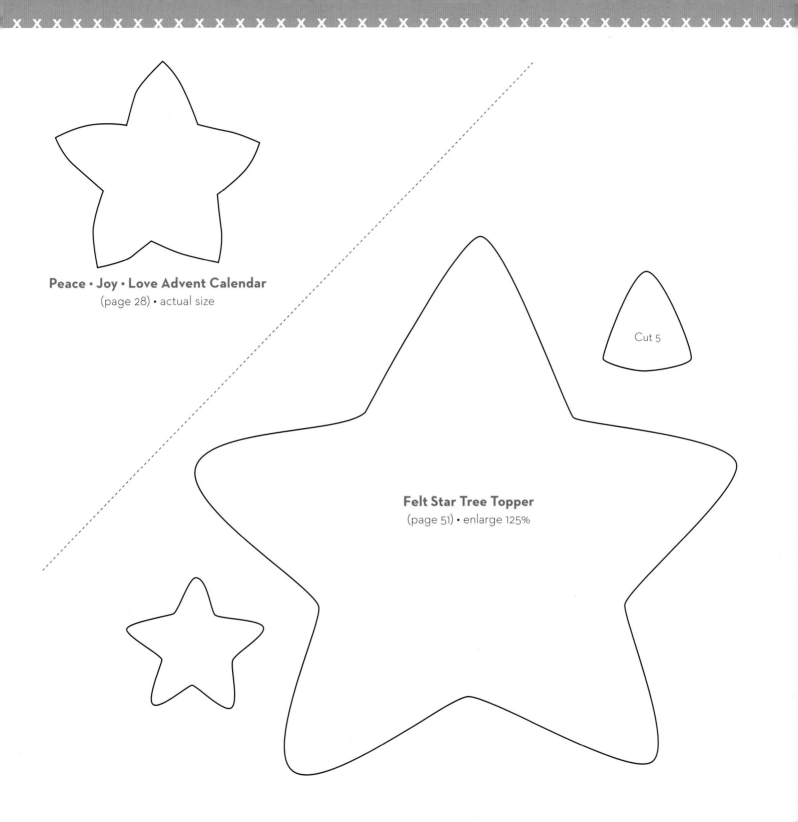

Peace • Joy • Love Advent Calendar
(page 28) • actual size

Cut 5

Felt Star Tree Topper
(page 51) • enlarge 125%

Soft Nativity

(page 44) • enlarge 200%

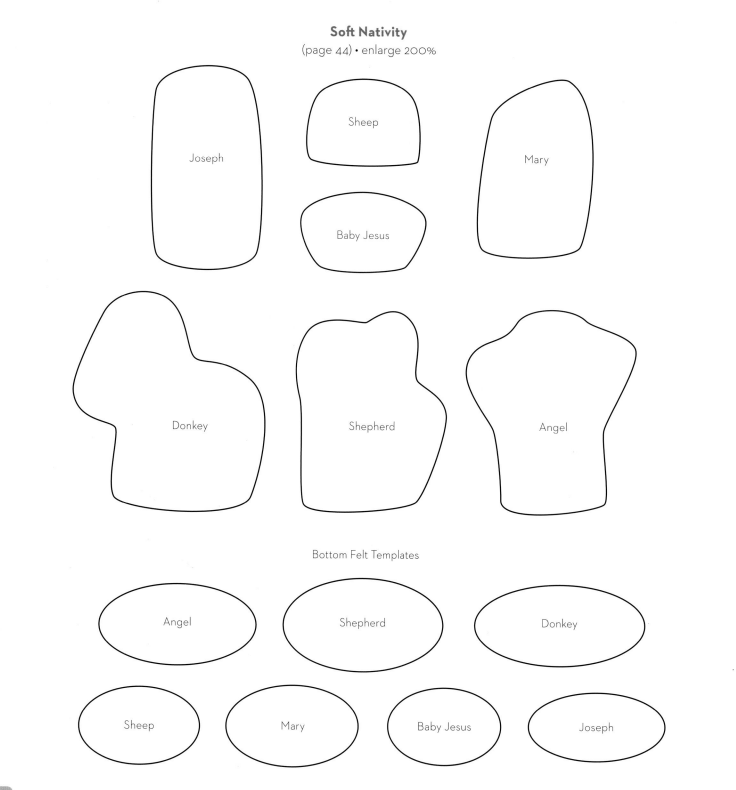

Joseph

Sheep

Mary

Baby Jesus

Donkey

Shepherd

Angel

Bottom Felt Templates

Angel

Shepherd

Donkey

Sheep

Mary

Baby Jesus

Joseph

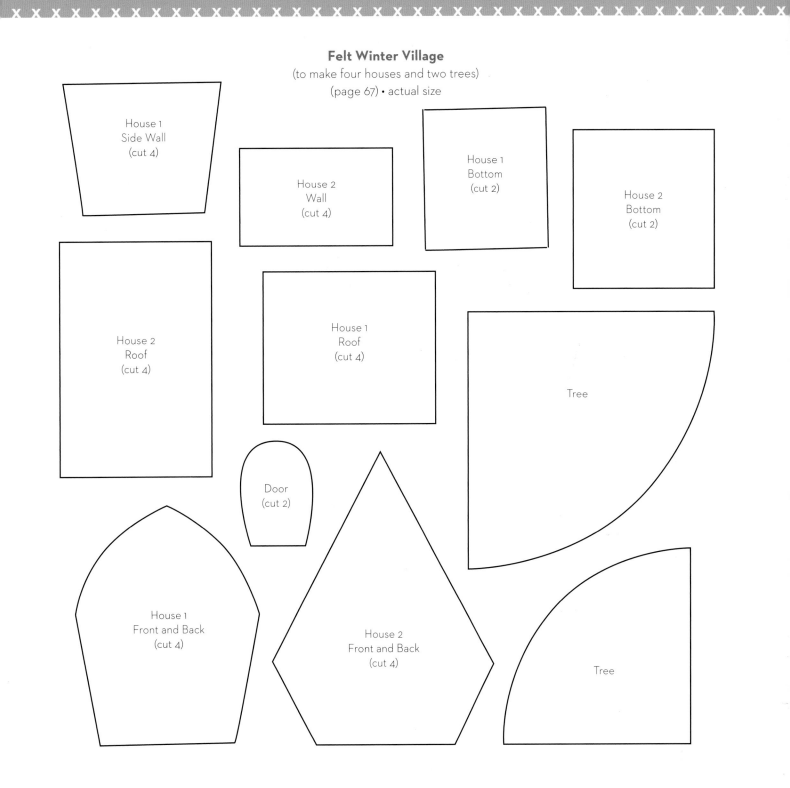

Felt Winter Village
(to make four houses and two trees)
(page 67) • actual size

House 1
Side Wall
(cut 4)

House 2
Wall
(cut 4)

House 1
Bottom
(cut 2)

House 2
Bottom
(cut 2)

House 2
Roof
(cut 4)

House 1
Roof
(cut 4)

Tree

Door
(cut 2)

House 1
Front and Back
(cut 4)

House 2
Front and Back
(cut 4)

Tree

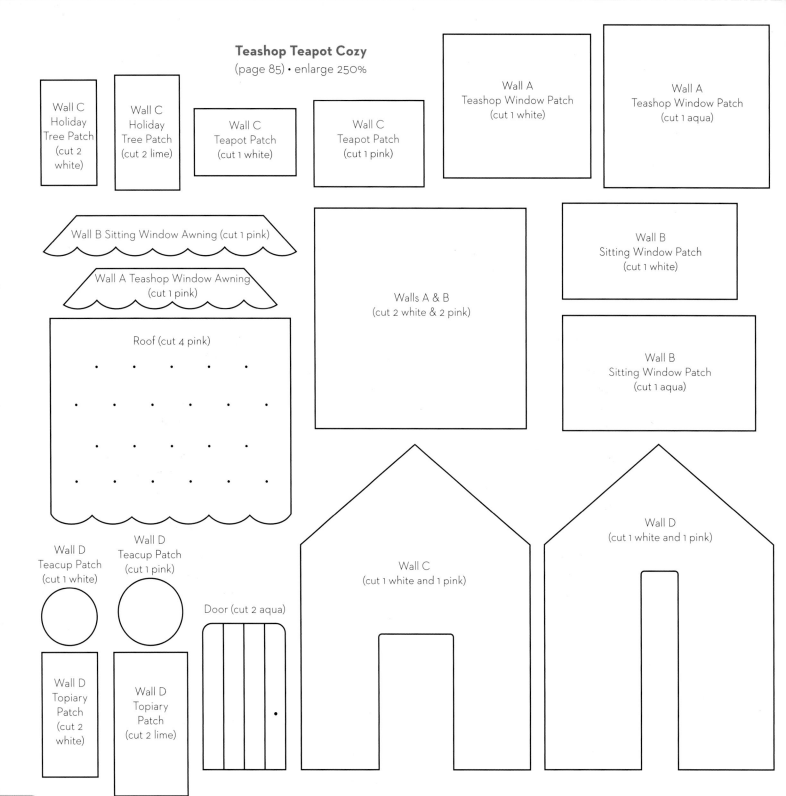

Teashop Teapot Cozy

(page 85) • enlarge 250%

Wall C Holiday Tree Patch (cut 2 white)

Wall C Holiday Tree Patch (cut 2 lime)

Wall C Teapot Patch (cut 1 white)

Wall C Teapot Patch (cut 1 pink)

Wall A Teashop Window Patch (cut 1 white)

Wall A Teashop Window Patch (cut 1 aqua)

Wall B Sitting Window Awning (cut 1 pink)

Wall A Teashop Window Awning (cut 1 pink)

Wall B Sitting Window Patch (cut 1 white)

Walls A & B (cut 2 white & 2 pink)

Wall B Sitting Window Patch (cut 1 aqua)

Roof (cut 4 pink)

Wall D Teacup Patch (cut 1 white)

Wall D Teacup Patch (cut 1 pink)

Door (cut 2 aqua)

Wall C (cut 1 white and 1 pink)

Wall D (cut 1 white and 1 pink)

Wall D Topiary Patch (cut 2 white)

Wall D Topiary Patch (cut 2 lime)

ABOUT THE DESIGNERS

John Q. Adams

John Q. Adams is a husband and father of three who, inspired by the growing number of crafting blogs and the emergence of vibrant, modern quilting fabrics in the textile industry, convinced his wife to teach him how to use her sewing machine. He started his popular blog, QuiltDad.com, in 2008 to share his love of patchwork with others. Today, John applies his modern quilting aesthetic by designing quilt patterns for both fabric designers and companies and contributing frequently to creative blogs, books, and other collaborative endeavors. John is also a co-founder of the popular e-magazine for modern quilters, *Fat Quarterly*. Born and raised in Brooklyn, New York, John currently lives in Holly Springs, North Carolina.

Carina Envoldsen-Harris

Carina Envoldsen-Harris is a designer, blogger, and author. Originally from Denmark, she now lives just outside London, UK, with her English husband. Carina has been making things for as long as she can remember—painting, drawing, and embroidering. Under the name Polka & Bloom, she creates colorful embroidery patterns and fabric designs. You can see more of her work in her book *Stitched Blooms* (Lark Crafts), and on her blog: carinascraftblog.com.

Laura Howard

Laura is a designer, crafter, and author who likes to make and do, and she is completely obsessed with felt! She's the author of two books about felt crafting: *Super-Cute Felt* and *Super-Cute Felt Animals*. Laura shares free tutorials and writes about her crafty adventures on her blog bugsandfishes.blogspot.com and sells her work at lupin.bigcartel.com.

Mollie Johanson

Mollie Johanson, the author of *Stitch Love: Sweet Creatures Big & Small* from Lark Crafts, has loved cute things, creative messes, and cuddly critters for as long as she can remember. Her blog at www.wildolive.blogspot.com is known for embroidery patterns, simply stitched projects, and playful printables, most often presenting charming creations with smiling faces. Her work has been featured on Mollie Makes, Australian Homespun, and in a variety of books, including several Lark Crafts titles.

Annie Kight

Armed with a glue gun at a very young age, Annie took her glittering very seriously. After many moons in a confectionery world she opted in for the life of a mini-sculptress. She daydreams a lot and rarely sleeps, which makes for a pie-in-the-sky kind of existence. You can find her pincushions, polymer clay pin-toppers, and dollhouse miniatures at etsy.com/shop/PinksAndNeedles, and keep up with her at her blog pinksandneedles.blogspot.com.

Teresa Mairal Barreu

Born and raised in Spain, Teresa Mairal Barreu learned knitting, crochet, and embroidery from her sewing, knitting, lace-making mother. After moving to Australia as an adult, and a long "craftless" spell, she caught the crafting bug again and became interested in patchwork and fabric. Now living in Paris, Teresa spends her spare time sewing and designing. When she's not sewing, she can be found drawing, painting, sculpting, embroidering, or felting. Her blog, Sewn Up by TeresaDownUnder, can be found at mypatchwork.wordpress.com.

ABOUT THE AUTHOR

Aimee Ray loves all types of art and crafts and is always trying something new. Besides embroidery, she dabbles in illustration, crochet, needle felting, sewing, and doll customizing. Aimee's home is in Northwest Arkansas where she has a view of the Ozark Mountains from her backyard. She lives with her husband, Josh, their son, and two big dogs.

Aimee has written three previous books of contemporary embroidery designs: *Doodle Stitching*; *Doodle Stitching: The Motif Collection*; *Doodle Stitching: Embroidery & Beyond*; and *Aimee Ray's Sweet & Simple Jewelry*. In addition, she has contributed to many other Lark titles. You can see more of her work at www.dreamfollow.com and follow her daily crafting endeavors at www.littledeartracks.blogspot.com.

ACKNOWLEDGMENTS

Doodle Stitching: The Holiday Motif Collection has been so much fun to work on, and these awesome people who helped make it possible deserve to be celebrated! Cheers to my husband, Josh, and my family who always encourage me in everything I do. Thank you to my mom, grandmas, and creative aunties who were always making something when I was growing up, and instilled a love of crafting in me. Many thanks to my wonderful editor, Kathy Sheldon; art director, Shannon Yokeley; and photographer, Cynthia Shaffer, for helping to make this book perfect. Many thanks to Beth Sweet and Amanda Carestio at Lark Books, and a special shout out to each of the super-talented designers who helped create the festive projects here!

CREDITS

Editors: Kathy Sheldon & Beth Sweet

Art Director: Shannon Yokeley

Illustrator: Aimee Ray

Photographer: Cynthia Shaffer

Cover Designer: Shannon Yokeley

INDEX